Contemporary
COOKING

Volume 5

Contemporary
COOKING

Volume 5

3M

Contemporary Cooking

**Editorial production by James Charlton Associates, Ltd.
New York. Editor-in-Chief, James Charlton; Managing
Editors, Barbara Binswanger, Jennie McGregor; Food
Editors, Inez M. Krech, Cecile Lamalle, Anne Lanigan,
Betsy Lawrence, Maria Robbins.**

**Book production and manufacturing consulting by:
Cobb/Dunlop Publishing Services, Inc., New York
Art Direction and interior design by:
Marsha Cohen/Parallelogram
Cover design by: Koechel/Peterson Design, Minneapolis**

**Acknowledgments: Allan Baillie, Pat Cocklin, Delu PAL
International, Aire deZanger, Alan Duns, John Elliott, Gus
Francisco, Melvin Grey, Gina Harris, Anthony Kay, Paul
Kemp, David Levin, David Meldrum, Roger Phillips, Nick
Powell, Iain Reid, John Turner, Paul Williams,
George Wright, Cuisinarts, Inc.**

Printed and bound in Yugoslavia by CGP Delo.

Library of Congress Cataloging in Publication Data
Main entry under title:

Contemporary Cooking.

Includes index.
1. Cookery. I. Minnesota Mining and Manufacturing
Company.
TX715.C7586   1984   641.5   84-2563
0-88159-500-4   —   (set)
ISBN: 0-88159–004–5

CONTENTS

for the Contemporary Cooking Series

VOLUME 5

Part One
PÂTÉS, TERRINES AND POTTED SPREADS

"A great deal is said and written about the innate cooking skill of every French housewife and every *patron-chef* of every other auberge, restaurant and transport café in the land. While not wishing in any way to belittle the culinary talents so lavishly bestowed by Providence upon the French, and so brilliantly cultivated by them, it should be observed that both housewife and restaurateur frequently lean heavily upon their local *charcutiers* and *pâtissiers*. If a housewife has but little time for cooking, she is able to rely upon the terrines and pâtés, the sausages, the hams and all the miscellaneous pork products of the *charcutier*, to make a quick midday meal for her family or a first course for her lunch party."

Elizabeth David
French Provincial Cooking

An amazing variety of takeout foods existed in France long before the first restaurant was opened. Pastrycooks had their *pâtisseries* for selling pastry; bread bakers had *boulangeries* where they sold bread; and pork butchers operated *charcuteries* where they sold savory preparations derived from the meat of the pig. Each profession had its own guild that jealously guarded rights, privileges and territory. Inevitably, disagreements arose as pork butchers, bakers and pastry chefs accused each other of overstepping their boundaries and trespassing on each other's trades. The *Larousse Gastronomique* tells us that "The main dispute between the pastry-cooks and the pork butchers, ending in a long court case, arose in connection with a ham pâté made by a man called Noël. The pâté in question was a ham, cooked as usual and enclosed in pastry. The pork butchers, quite rightly, maintained that as the crust did not adhere to the ham it could not be considered a pie. It is true that only raw ingredients enclosed in pastry and cooked at the same time as the pastry can be considered as pies. The pork butchers, therefore, won their case."

Today we make little or no distinction between pâtés, terrines or even smooth, savory pastes of liver or even fish. Almost any meat or fish mixture that is baked in the oven can be called a pâté or terrine, although sometimes a distinction is made (not strictly accurately) between a smooth mixture which is generally called a pâté and firmer, coarser and layered mixtures, called terrines.

To be accurate, the word pâté (which means pie) should be used only to describe a meat or fish mixture which is completely enclosed in pastry and baked in the oven. In other words, a pie. Nowadays, this dish or type of pâté is termed *pâté en croûte.*

A terrine takes its name from the oblong oven-proof earthenware or china dish in which the coarsely cut mixture of meats is cooked. A terrine is always made from raw materials and baked in the oven. It is traditionally decorated with bay leaves laid in a trefoil pattern (an arrangement of three leaves) on top.

Pâtés and terrines, as we know them, are well-seasoned meat or fish mixtures, not enclosed in pastry, which have been baked in the oven, usually in a dish lined with bacon or pork fat. The consistency of these mixtures can vary from the velvety smooth to the coarse and crumbly. A smooth pâté mixture must be exactly that, as smooth as velvet and rich and creamy. The most famous pâté of this type is the classic *pâté de foie gras. Foie gras* is the liver of a goose which has been forcibly fed on a diet of corn mash. The two related breeds of *foie gras* goose are the Toulouse and the Strasbourg, both much larger than the common farmyard goose. The intensive diet causes the liver to swell so that one liver can weigh as much as 3 pounds.

Fresh *foie gras* is highly prized for its flavor and richness and is extremely expensive. The pâté made from it often includes truffles and vintage Cognac, so that the resulting product is among the costliest of luxury foods.

Superb special pâtés can be made without such expensive ingredients as *foie gras* and truffles. Various cuts of pork, duck, pheasant, veal, chicken and rabbit produce some of the finest pâtés, as do their livers, which can be prepared on their own or used to flavor a composed pâté.

Great chefs cherish their special recipes for these preparations, and over the centuries many famous pâté recipes have evolved. It is said that people used to stand on line for hours outside M. Talleyrand's kitchen hoping for a chance to buy the remainders of pâtés cooked by the great Carême.

In France, where the making of pâtés and terrines has developed into a fine art, most villages have their own recipes for a local *pâté de campagne* (hearty country-style pâté), sold by the *charcuterie,* and many restaurants proudly serve their own *pâté maison* (house pâté).

Closely related to pâtés and terrines are the potted meats and fish pastes which are a specialty of English cooks, and the *rillons, rillettes* and *rillauds* of France. *Rillons, rillettes* and *rillauds* are all made of highly seasoned bits of pork that have been cooked in lard, slowly and for a long time, then potted in the same fat they were cooked in. The difference among the three products lies in the consistency of the paste (*rillettes,* for example, are shredded and pounded) and the size of the pieces of pork.

In Britain, potting was developed as a method of preserving pieces of meat and fish that were not immediately needed. All potted meats and pastes were intended to last for several weeks, enabling cooks in large households to prepare a large quantity in advance and so to be able to serve delicious meat and fish dishes at times of the year when the only other sort available was salted and dried.

Pâtés, terrines and potted meats and fish rank among the most delicious and useful creations to emerge from the kitchen. Although some of the layered and checkered pâtés require time and patience on the part of the cook, none of them is difficult to make and almost all are better when made several days before serving.

Almost all terrines and pâtés call for a basic mixture of forcemeat (usually finely ground pork, or a mixture of pork and veal) in which other flavorful meats and special ingredients are embedded or layered. The dark meat of ducks, geese and game birds is popular and traditional in a pâté of this sort. Often the meat is marinated for several hours or longer in a mixture of Cognac or fortified wine such as port, sherry or Madeira and herbs.

The classical French spice mixture called *quatre épices* ("four spices," although often there are more) is used to season the forcemeat. Another spice mixture often used is *sel épicé* (spiced salt).

Mushrooms, truffles, pistachios and even greens like spinach or chard can be added to the terrine for extra flavor, texture and visual interest.

An exciting and delicious culinary evolution has come about with the development of terrines composed entirely of vegetables. These are lighter both in flavor and in calories and have become very popular served just as traditional pâtés are—as hors d'oeuvre, first course, light lunch or picnic food.

PÂTÉS AND TERRINES

If you can make a meat loaf, you can make terrines and pâtés to rival any you might find in restaurants or specialty stores, many of them costing upwards of ten dollars a pound.

While some pâtés or terrines are made of just one kind of liver, meat, poultry, game or fish, it is more common to use a mixture of ingredients.

The mixture of ingredients may be plain or fancy. Plain pâtés are made of a forcemeat flavored with herbs and spices and then baked in a slow oven. Fancy pâtés have strips of meat—fillets of duck breast, veal, ham, tongue—and sometimes pieces of truffle, mushrooms or pistachios sandwiched between the layers of the forcemeat to form an attractive pattern when the pâté is sliced.

All meat pâtés benefit from being made several days in advance so that the flavors can blend and mature. Fish pâtés, however, and most vegetable pâtés do not keep as well and should be eaten within 2 or 3 days.

Making Textured and Layered Pâtés

Ingredients. The basic forcemeat mixture can be made of a variety of meats but almost always includes pork, and the entire mixture should contain about half as much fat as lean meat. Because American pork is much leaner than its European counterpart, it may be necessary to ask your butcher to grind some extra pork fat into the mixture. The fat keeps the pâté from drying out as it cooks by basting it from the inside. It also adds flavor and keeping qualities.

You will need additional pork fat or bacon to line, or bard, the terrine or baking dish in which the pâté is cooked. If fresh pork fat is hard to get, you can use bacon or salt pork, but both should be blanched for 5 to 10 minutes to remove excess salt and heavy smoky flavor.

The forcemeat is often flavored with minced onions, mushrooms, shallots or garlic. All of these should be sautéed in a little butter until soft before adding them to the forcemeat.

Although most forcemeat mixtures are ground in a meat grinder by a butcher, you will have better control over the final product and achieve better texture if you prepare your own forcemeat. A food processor is ideal because it allows you to get a variety of textures, leaving some of the meat in larger chunks.

Even more traditional is to chop the meat by hand with a large sharp knife and incorporate the fat as you chop.

A binding agent is sometimes used to make a crumbly or soft forcemeat mixture firm enough for slicing when it is cold. There are various binding agents such as eggs, good jellied stock, butter, bread crumbs or *panades* made of flour or rice.

Strips of boneless lean meat can be layered in the pâté for added texture and flavor. Among the many possible choices, you can consider veal, ham, tongue, rabbit, chicken, duck, goose, pheasant, or any other game bird. The meat should be removed from the bone, completely skinned, and cut into 1/2-inch-wide strips. The meat should then rest in a flavorful marinade for several hours or overnight. These ingredients will give a clearly visible pattern when the pâté is sliced.

Any leftover bits of meat and fat should be chopped up or ground and incorporated into the forcemeat mixture.

Seasoning a Pâté. Seasoning plays an important role in the final taste. The seasoning must be carefully adjusted before the pâté is cooked. It is important to keep in mind that as the pâté will be served cold the intensity of seasoning should be increased. A cold dish always requires more salt, pepper and other herbs and spices than a warm one.

To check salt, pepper and other flavorings, fry a small spoonful of the forcemeat in a little unsalted butter; taste and adjust accordingly.

Never taste uncooked forcemeat that contains raw pork.

Herbs and Spices. Many different herbs and spices are used to flavor pâtés, including thyme, tarragon, chervil, bay leaves, allspice, black, white and sometimes green peppercorns, and nutmeg.

Many French cooks rely on a seasoning mixture called *quatre épices,* a blend of 4 spices: pepper, nutmeg, cloves and either ginger or cinnamon. Spiced salt *(sel épicé)* is another favorite: a mixture of salt with 6 or 7 ground spices.

A *bouquet garni* (bay leaf, thyme and parsley) is often added to *rillettes* as they are cooking.

Juniper berries give a distinctive flavor to poultry and game pâtés, while orange rind can add a lively note of fragrance and aroma to a duck-based pâté.

Bay leaves are almost always included, either crumbled into the forcemeat mixture or placed whole on top to make an attractive pattern.

Wines and Spirits. Strongly flavored alcoholic spirits are often used in pâtés both to add moisture and to impart extra flavor. Fine brandies, sherry, Madeira, port, and even bourbon can all be used to good advantage.

Truffles. A truffle is a fungus that grows underground. Dogs and pigs are trained to sniff them out. Because they are difficult to find, they are very expensive. When they are in season, specialty stores will occasionally have fresh truffles for sale. Otherwise they can be bought in cans.

Truffles vary in color depending on the type; the best known are the black truffles from Périgord in France. White Italian truffles, however, are becoming better known in this country. Truffles always add a touch of luxury to a pâté, as they have a unique and wonderful aroma. When they are coarsely chopped they help to make an attractive speckled pattern. If you are using canned truffles, be sure to add the liquid from the can to the forcemeat.

Pistachio Nuts. Pistachios are often added to pâtés for their rich, nutty taste, crisp texture and unusual green color. Avoid using pistachios that have been dyed red.

Assembling the Pâté. Have ready the following:

The forcemeat, seasoned and mixed with sautéed aromatic vegetables (onions, garlic, etc.) and any other special ingredients such as truffles, pistachios, spirits.

The pieces of meat for layering, cut into thin boneless strips, and seasoned and marinated.

Strips of fresh pork fat or bacon blanched or salt pork, to line the baking dish or terrine.

Cooking the Pâté. The top of the terrine should be well sealed with heavy aluminum foil. Then set the terrine into a larger baking dish or roasting pan into which you will pour enough boiling water to reach halfway up the sides of the terrine. However, different recipes may call for more or less water around the terrine.

Place in a preheated 350°F oven and bake for the amount of time stated in the specific recipe. Check the level of water from time to time and add more hot water to the roasting pan when it is needed.

Finishing the Pâté. Most pâtés are meant to be eaten cold and they should be allowed to rest a day or so until the flavors have fully blended and mellowed. A cooled pâté should wait for at least 24 hours before being eaten.

Be sure to allow the pâté to cool completely after baking, before setting it in the refrigerator to chill. If the pâté will be served directly from its baking dish, cover it tightly with clean aluminum foil, set it in a pan of cold water until it is quite cold, and then refrigerate until needed.

A pâté that is to be turned out of its dish before serving must be firm and sliceable. To ensure this, it must be pressed while cooling. Place a piece of

foil-covered cardboard, cut to fit inside the rim, on the surface of the pâté. Stand the dish in a pan of cold water. Weight the pâté with kitchen weights or unopened canned goods or other suitable articles. Leave the pâté until quite cold, then remove from the pan of water and refrigerate. Leave the weight in place if there is room in your refrigerator.

Serving a cooked pâté or terrine. If the pâté is to be turned out and sliced, run a knife around the dish to loosen the pâté and its jacket of bacon or fat. Lay a plate over the dish and invert plate and dish together. The turned-out pâté needs no further garnish, except maybe a sprig of parsley or watercress on top to add a touch of color.

A pâté to be served from its dish can be decorated in several ways. It can have the traditional 3 bay leaves which must be added before baking. Alternatively, a cooled pâté which has had the covering fat removed and its surface browned can be covered with a small amount of liquid aspic before it is refrigerated. Decorations, such as orange slices, a fanned gherkin and juniper berries, can be set in the aspic, which will become jellied as the pâté cools.

Storing Pâtés. Most pâtés should be made at least a day or two in advance to allow the mixture to mature and the full flavor of all the ingredients to blend together. A pâté that has not matured will not have a well-developed flavor.

Meat pâtés left in their containers will keep for a week. If properly sealed, they will keep in the refrigerator for up to 5 weeks.

For longer storage, remove pâté from its dish and scrape away every bit of aspic that has formed around it. (This aspic will turn sour long before the pâté begins to go bad.) Then return the pâté to its clean dish and cover with melted lard or clarified butter to a depth of ½ inch; cover with plastic wrap and return to refrigerator. Or simply wrap pâté well with plastic wrap and refrigerate. Either way, the pâté will keep for up to a month.

Pâtés may be frozen although this is not recommended. When frozen, they lose flavor and the texture is softened.

Fish pâtés and vegetable pâtés do not keep well and should be eaten within 3 days.

Making Smooth Pâtés and Savory Spreads

Although smooth pâtés and spreads with their velvety textures are every bit as delicious and luxurious as the layered terrines, they are considerably quicker to make. Some smooth pâtés, like the Danish Liver Pâté, are baked in the oven in a manner similar to the layered pâtés; many others are not cooked after assembling, but beforehand. Chicken Liver Pâté and many fish pâtés are prepared by cooking the separate ingredients briefly and then either pounding them together or reducing them to a paste in a food processor or blender.

Ingredients. The principal ingredient must be either fish (fresh, canned or smoked) or a meat that needs very little cooking, such as chicken livers, duck livers, etc.

As with other pâtés, smooth pâtés and spreads nearly always contain minced onion, garlic, shallots and other aromatic flavorings. They should also be well seasoned, as they are usually served cold, and cold reduces the strength of seasoning.

Fats are used in the form of butter, oil, lard or cream cheese. The fats are used both in cooking the ingredients and as an addition to the mixture as it is being pounded or processed.

Preparing the Pâté. Remove any sinew, gristle, skin or bones from the fish or meat. Then cook according to the instructions of the specific recipe. Usually the meat or fish is sautéed in butter or oil along with the minced garlic, onions and other flavoring ingredients. Brandy or wine may be added towards the end along with the herbs and spices.

Use a food processor or blender to make a smooth paste. The mixture

Checkered Game Pâté

This recipe uses pheasant, but any game bird can be used in the same way, or even domestic poultry. A pheasant weighing 1¼ pounds will yield about 9 ounces of meat. For this recipe you need 1 pound of boned game meat.

This recipe can be halved to make a smaller pâté. To make it more economical, substitute mushrooms for the truffles.

The flavor of the pâté will be improved if it is allowed to mature in the refrigerator for a few days.

14 portions

1	pound boned pheasant meat
1	ounce sliced truffles
¼	cup brandy
1	tablespoon butter
1	shallot or small onion
12	ounces boneless fresh veal
12	ounces boneless fresh lean pork
12	ounces boneless pork belly, without rind
1	ounce shelled pistachios
2	large eggs
½	cup Madeira wine
	salt and black pepper
½	teaspoon crumbled dried thyme
½	teaspoon ground allspice
12	ounces fresh pork fatback
2	bay leaves

1 Cut the boned breast meat into neat ½-inch strips and put in a dish with truffles and brandy. Reserve truffle liquid.

5 Add pistachios. Beat eggs and Madeira and add to minced mixture. Add salt and pepper to taste, thyme and allspice.

6 Mix well. Sauté a spoonful of the forcemeat in unsalted butter and check seasoning. Add more if needed.

7 Cut fatback into ¼-inch slices, then into long strips. Preheat oven to 350°F.

11 Press a third of the forcemeat in the bottom of the terrine. Smooth the top to make it level.

12 Put half of the breast strips and truffles neatly along the length of the terrine. Add a few strips of fatback.

13 Cover with half of remaining forcemeat. Add remaining breast strips, truffles and a few more strips of fatback.

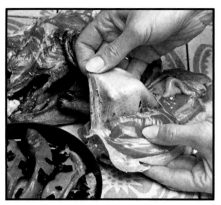

2 Remove as much meat as possible from the pheasant carcasses. Reserve the livers. Discard all skin.

3 Melt the butter. Peel and mince shallot or onion and sauté in the butter with the livers until both are soft.

4 Chop all the meat except breast strips and fatback. Add sautéed onion and livers to the meat and mince the entire mixture.

8 Lay strips of fatback, parallel to each other, across the bottom of a 2-quart terrine.

9 Repeat at right angles to form a lattice pattern in the terrine. Press strips on the sides as well.

10 Drain breast strips and truffles. Add the brandy marinade and truffle liquid to forcemeat and mix well.

14 Cover with remaining forcemeat. Add a lattice of fatback on top and place the bay leaves in the center.

15 Cover the terrine with foil. Pierce a hole for steam to escape. Cook in a water bath in the oven for 2½ to 3 hours.

16 Cover with foil-covered cardboard and put weights on top. When cold, turn out and remove excess fat.

Pork-Liver Pâté

12 portions

- 1 pound pork liver
- 6 ounces smoked bacon
- 12 ounces fresh pork belly
- 6 ounces fresh pork fatback
- 1 garlic clove
- 6 tablespoons medium-dry white wine
- 1 tablespoon brandy
  salt and pepper
  pinch of grated mace
- 1 large egg
- 2 tablespoons flour
- 1 tablespoon lard
- 14 ounces fresh pork fat for barding

1 Wash the liver and pat dry. Chop liver, bacon, pork belly and fatback, then mince. Peel and mince the garlic.

2 Mix minced ingredients and garlic. Pour in the wine and brandy and refrigerate overnight.

6 Lay fat strips across the greased pan, overlapping them slightly and pressing them against the greased surfaces.

7 The strips should line the pan completely so that in baking they surround the pâté mixture on all sides.

8 Turn the mixture into the pan and cover the top with remaining strips of barding fat, cut to fit. Cover tightly with foil.

10 When cooked, remove pâté from oven and from pan of water. Test with a skewer; if pâté is ready, it should come out clean.

11 Remove foil and lay foil-wrapped cardboard, cut to size, over the pâté. Weight it with cans.

12 Put dish in a pan of cold water overnight. Remove weights and cardboard, cover with plastic wrap, and refrigerate 24 hours.

3 Season well with salt and pepper; add the mace. Beat the egg into the flour and add to the mixture. Mix well by hand.

4 Preheat oven to 350°F. Use the lard to grease a 6-cup loaf pan or oblong baking dish.

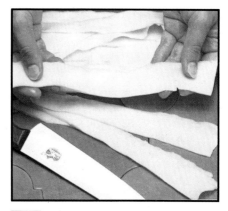

5 Cut barding fat into 1½-inch strips and cut strips into ¼-inch-thick slices. Reserve some strips for the top.

OR If not turning out the pâté, press it into the greased baking dish, cover the surface with fat, and cover dish with foil.

8 Bake as directed in step 9, but after 2 hours remove foil, and fat too if wished, and brown in the oven for remaining baking time.

9 Put the dish in a roasting pan with water halfway up the sides of the dish. Bake for 2½ hours, until juices run clear.

13 To serve, remove plastic wrap and all surface fat. Run a knife around the edges to loosen the pâté and fat coating.

14 Place a plate over the baking dish and invert both together. Serve the pâté sliced, with crusty bread.

OR To serve from the dish, cut pâté into wedges with a knife; if it is crumbly, spoon it out.

may be quite liquid while it is still warm, but will turn solid as it cools.

If you do not have a food processor or blender, pound the ingredients in a mortar with a pestle, or press them through a sieve, until well blended and completely smooth.

Whichever method you choose, the next step is to taste the pâté and adjust the seasonings.

Pour the mixture into a decorative pot or container, tapping the bottom against a hard countertop to release any air bubbles. Wipe the rim of the pot clean and cover tightly with plastic wrap. Let cool and refrigerate the pâté until it is thoroughly chilled and firm.

The pâté may be served in its pot with a spreading knife and bread and crackers.

Potted Meats and Pastes

Potted meats and pastes are similar in taste and texture to pâtés but they are made with meats and fish that have already been cooked. However, *rillettes* (French potted pork) are made with raw pork, which is then baked for a long time.

Potting is, literally, pressing food

Potted Beef

3 or 4 appetizer portions

10	tablespoons clarified butter
7	ounces cold roast beef
2	ounces cooked ham

pinch of grated mace
salt and black pepper

1 Melt 4 tablespoons clarified butter. Trim skin, fat, gristle and sinew from beef and ham. Chop roughly.

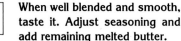

5 When well blended and smooth, taste it. Adjust seasoning and add remaining melted butter.

6 Place three or four 4-ounce pots on a wooden surface. Melt remaining clarified butter.

7 Press the meat paste into the pots with the back of a spoon. Tap pots to release air bubbles.

into pots and sealing the pots with butter or other fat. The method could not be simpler and it is an excellent way of using up a small quantity of leftover meat or fish.

Ingredients. Any kind of meat, poultry or game can be potted but mild-flavored white meats, such as chicken and veal, are more interesting if mixed with a small quantity of a more strong-flavored meat and some spices. Chicken or turkey is often potted with ham or bacon, for instance, an excellent way of using leftover roast chicken or Christmas turkey. Be most careful, though, when using a meat that has been cooked with a stuffing. All traces of the stuffing must be removed as it is more liable to spoil and could taint the meat, making it dangerous to eat.

When using cooked leftovers, bear in mind that roasted or grilled meat is best for potting. Stewed meat usually contains too much liquid and will not blend well with the butter.

Whether you use leftover meat or freshly cooked meat, it must be quite cold before being potted. Even tepid meat will melt the butter slightly and the two will not blend well together.

2 Chop or shred the meat in a food processor; or put it through a meat grinder fitted with the fine blade.

3 Pour 2 tablespoons of the melted butter into a bowl and with a wooden spoon mix it with the meat and the seasonings.

4 Reduce the mixture to a paste, a little at a time, in a food processor or in a mortar with a pestle.

8 Leave ½-inch space at the top of each pot for the butter. Smooth surface of the paste and wipe the rims of the pots.

9 Trickle in enough melted butter to coat the surface. Tilt and rotate the pots and leave for the butter to set. Keep pan of butter in a warm place.

10 When butter has set, trickle in another layer and leave to set until firm. Label pots, cover with foil, and refrigerate.

Strong-flavored fish, such as smoked fish and varieties of oily fish, make the best pastes. The delicate flavor of fresh white fish is lost when it is blended with the butter.

Butter is as important to potted meat pastes as the main ingredient. It moistens and flavors the cooked flesh which would otherwise dry out, helps to preserve it and, finally, seals it from attack by germs in the air.

The butter must be unsalted and it must be clarified before use. (See below.) If the recipe does not give a specific quantity, use the following guidelines to help you: Most meat and fish are mixed with a quarter to a third of their weight in butter and in some cases the ratio is 50:50. You will also need extra butter for sealing the pots after they have been filled.

For fat meat, such as pork and ham, and combinations of meat containing fat meat allow a sixth to a quarter the weight of meat in butter. Beef, lamb, duck and oily fish: allow a quarter to a third the weight of the meat or fish in butter. Dry meat and fish, such as veal, poultry, game, salmon and white fish: allow a third to half the weight of the meat or fish in butter, or more if necessary.

Sealing the pots: Allow 1 to 2 tablespoons butter to cover a pot 4 inches in diameter, and up to 4 tablespoons butter for a pot 6 inches across.

Herbs, spices and seasonings: The traditional flavorings, proved most successful through long use, are thyme, mace and bay leaf. This is one instance where it is usually better to use dried rather than fresh herbs. They are easier to blend in and their total lack of moisture means there is less likelihood of their developing bad flavors.

Potted meats and pastes need to be well seasoned with salt and pepper because the butter mollifies the flavor of the meat or fish. A few grains of cayenne pepper are often used. Go carefully with the salt when using smoked or salt fish and, when making fish paste, remember that a few drops of lemon juice always improve the flavor.

Other spices and flavorings such as nutmeg, anchovy essence or Worcestershire sauce are used, especially with more strong-flavored meat, for variety's sake. About ½ teaspoon essence or sauce is sufficient to flavor 2 tablespoons butter, but always taste the product as you go along and increase the flavoring if necessary.

Potting is both quick and easy. It can be divided into 4 stages: clarifying the butter; preparing the meat or fish; pounding or blending the ingredients; and filling and sealing the pots.

Clarified Butter. You will need a large quantity of clarified butter, as it is both blended with the main ingredient and used to seal the pots once they have been filled. Using clarified butter is most important, as plain butter could easily go rancid because of the milk still retained in it. It is not difficult to clarify butter and using it ensures that the potted meat or fish paste tastes and looks delicious. It sets a deep golden seal on the pot, quite different from the cloudier and less golden color of plain melted butter.

If the butter is prepared in ad-vance, remove it to room temperature before preparing the meat or fish.

Preparing the Meat or Fish. The meat or fish should already be cooked, but if you are cooking specifically for potting, it is preferable to broil the food. Cool it as quickly as possible by putting it in a chilled container and stand this in a bowl of iced water. Do not put a lid on the container or the evaporation will drip back onto the food. The food is ready for use when it reaches room temperature.

The food should be as pure as possible. Trim any skin, gristle and sinew from meat, or skin and bones from fish. Scrape any crumbs, sauce or batter from fish if it has been coated previously. Drain canned fish thoroughly.

Using a food processor: if you intend to use a food processor to mix the meat with the butter, chop or shred the meat. Fish should be flaked and any hairlike bones that appear should be removed.

Weigh out the amount of butter needed for mixing with the food. Soft-

Clarified Butter

 1 Place amount of butter needed in a heavy saucepan over low heat. When melted, spoon off the foam on top.

2 Pour butter through a sieve lined with cheesecloth, leaving the milky residue behind.

en this with the back of a wooden spoon so that it will blend more easily with the food. Do not melt it as this ruins its blending qualities. If it is already melted, let it cool until soft.

At this stage a food processor or blender will make your work much easier. In a bowl, mix the chopped meat or flaked fish with the chosen herbs or flavorings and the smallest quantity of clarified butter recommended. Process the mixture, a small quantity at a time, in the processor or blender until the butter is fully blended in and the paste is smooth.

Pounding by hand: if you have no food processor or blender, mince meat with a chef's knife on a sturdy board 2 or 3 times. Remove bones from fish, mash it well, then sieve it.

Weigh ingredients if necessary and calculate the quantity of clarified butter. Soften the butter with a spoon. Mix the food with the flavorings and the smallest recommended quantity of clarified butter, in a mortar. Pound the ingredients with a pestle until they are well mixed and the paste is as smooth as you can make it. Taste the product before removing it from the container

in which it was blended. Add more butter and/or flavorings if you think they are needed.

Filling the Pots. Put the pots on a firm surface, such as a wooden board or table. If you are using glass or stoneware pots, do not put them on a metal surface. While you are filling them, you will need to tap them against the surface fairly hard to make sure they are filling properly, and if they are glass or ceramic they may crack or break.

Roughly chop the clarified butter that is needed for sealing. Put it in a small heavy saucepan and melt it slowly over gentle heat. Remove butter from heat as soon as melted and set aside while you fill the pots.

Press the meat or fish mixture into the pots with the back of a spoon. Tap the bottom of the pot sharply against the surface at least twice while filling, to release any air bubbles. Leave at least ½ inch of headspace above the level of the mixture. Smooth the surface and wipe the rim of the pot clean with kitchen paper.

Trickle just enough melted butter over the pots to cover the surface and seal in the potted mixture. Tilt and ro-

tate the pots slightly to make sure that the butter covers the entire surface. Put the pan of unused butter in a warm place so that it will not solidify. Leave the pots, without disturbing them, until the butter topping is firm. Then trickle over a second layer of butter. Tilt and rotate the pots again and leave to set firmly. When completely set, label the pots carefully and cover with plastic wrap or foil to prevent the butter drying out. Store in the refrigerator.

Storage. Homemade potted meats and fish pastes will keep safely for several days in a refrigerator but should not be thought of as long-term preserves. For safety, use a product that has been made with freshly cooked meat or fish within 4 days, and one made from leftover precooked food within 3 days.

The potted meat or paste should be served at room temperature. Remove it from the refrigerator an hour or two before serving. Once it has reached room temperature do not attempt to chill it again, even if the butter seal has not been broken. Once removed from the refrigerator it must all be used.

Smooth Liver Pâté

8 portions

1 pound, 2 ounces, calf's liver or poultry livers
4 ounces smoked bacon
1 small onion
5 tablespoons butter
2 hard-cooked eggs

pinch of dried mixed herbs
1 tablespoon brandy
2 tablespoons heavy cream
salt and pepper
watercress sprigs

Chop the liver and bacon by hand or in a food processor until fine. Peel and mince the onion. Mix meats and onion together. Preheat oven to 350°F. Melt 4 tablespoons of the butter in a heavy skillet. Fry the meat and onion mixture gently for about 4 minutes, turning the mixture to brown all over. Remove pan from heat.

Peel and chop the hard-cooked eggs. Add them to the meat and pound the mixture to a smooth paste in a mortar, or return to the food processor, in batches, and process until smooth. Mix in the herbs, brandy and cream and season to taste. Grease a 4-cup baking dish with remaining tablespoon

of butter. Press the mixture firmly into the dish, leaving no air pockets. Cover dish securely with foil. Set in a pan of very hot water and bake for 40 to 50 minutes.

Remove pâté from oven, check to make sure it is cooked, and remove from the pan of water. Take off the foil and cover with a sheet of wax paper. Stand the dish in a pan of cold water in a cool place until quite cold. Cover pâté again with foil or plastic wrap and refrigerate for at least 24 hours. To serve, slice or spoon from the dish and garnish each portion with watercress sprigs.

Chicken-Liver Pâté

4 appetizer portions

1 small onion
1 garlic clove
8 ounces chicken livers
4 tablespoons lightly salted
     butter
1 tablespoon brandy

1 tablespoon port or Madeira wine
1 teaspoon Dijon-style mustard
     pinch of grated mace
     salt and pepper
3 tablespoons jellied chicken
     consommé

Peel and chop onion and garlic. Mince onion and put garlic through a press. Wash chicken livers, drain and pat dry. Discard any connective tissue. Melt 2 tablespoons of the butter in a skillet. Put in onion and garlic and sauté until soft. Warm remaining butter. Add chicken livers to the skillet and cook gently, turning them now and then, for 6 minutes. Livers should be brown but not crisp. Scrape contents of the skillet into a mixing bowl. Pour brandy and wine into the skillet and deglaze it over moderate heat. Pour the deglazing into the bowl of livers. Add the softened butter, the mustard and mace. Season well with salt and pepper. Mash or pound the mixture, or purée it in batches in a food processor, until completely smooth. If you mash or pound it, put it through a sieve afterward to make it smooth.

Taste the pâté and add extra seasoning if needed. Press into an attractive earthenware pot, about 1½-cup size. Tap the pot sharply to make the pâté settle and release air bubbles. Do not fill the dish quite full; leave at least ½-inch headspace. Cover pâté with wax paper and refrigerate until firm.

When pâté is firm and cold, melt enough of the consommé to cover it; the amount depends on the shape of the pot. When consommé is cool but still liquid but almost on the point of setting, spoon it over the pâté. Leave the pot in a cool place until consommé is set. Cover the pot with plastic wrap but do not let the wrap touch the jellied layer. Refrigerate for 24 hours. Use within the next 2 days. Serve from the dish with a spoon. Accompany with thin dry toast.

Liver Sausage with Orange

6 appetizer portions

4	ounces unsalted butter	½	teaspoon black pepper
12	ounces good-quality liver sausage	1	teaspoon salt
1	garlic clove	1	tablespoon orange juice
¼	cup medium-dry sherry	1	teaspoon grated orange rind
2	tablespoons heavy cream	3	orange slices

Put the butter in a mixing bowl and cream it with a wooden spoon until soft but not melted. Add the liver sausage. Peel garlic and put through a press into the mixture. Add sherry, cream, pepper, salt, orange juice and rind. Beat the ingredients together until well combined. Spoon the mixture into 6 individual ramekins, 4-ounce size. Halve the orange slices and garnish each ramekin with an orange piece. Set the dishes in the refrigerator to chill for 30 minutes before serving.

Pâté Maison

12 portions

1	tablespoon lard	¼	cup soft white bread crumbs
10	strips of smoked bacon	1	large egg
4	ounces pork liver	1	tablespoon milk
4	ounces fresh pork belly	6	tablespoons brandy
8	ounces cooked rabbit, cold		salt and pepper
8	ounces pork sausage meat		
1	onion		

Grease a 5-cup round or oval baking dish with the lard and line it with 7 bacon strips. Keep remaining 3 strips to cover the top. Preheat oven to 350°F.

Remove any sinew, skin, gristle or bone from the liver, pork belly and rabbit. Chop liver and pork and shred the rabbit. Put meats in a large bowl, add sausage, and mix thoroughly. Peel and chop the onion and add to the meats with the bread crumbs. Mix together egg, milk and brandy. Pour this into the meat and stir in well. Season to taste and mix again. Turn the mixture into the lined dish. Cover with reserved bacon strips. Cover the dish tightly with foil. Stand it in a roasting pan with water halfway up the sides of the pâté dish. Bake for 1½ hours.

Check to see that pâté is done. Remove from oven and take off the foil cover. Cover pâté with a foil-covered cardboard cut to fit the dish. Stand weights on top. Set the dish in a pan of cold water and leave in a cold place overnight.

Take off weight and cardboard. Scrape off any excess fat around the edges. Refrigerate pâté for 12 hours. Remove bacon strips. Turn pâté out for serving.

Spinach and Sausage Pâté

12 portions

1½	pounds fresh pork fatback	1	rosemary sprig
2½	pounds fresh spinach	4	to 6 chive leaves
	salt and pepper	½	teaspoon dried marjoram
2	onions	½	teaspoon dried savory
2	garlic cloves	2	large eggs
2	ounces cooked ham	1½	pounds sausage meat
8	ounces smoked bacon	2	tablespoons lard
1	parsley sprig		

Have the butcher cut the fatback into thin slices. Wash the spinach thoroughly; pull off any coarse or damaged leaves and all coarse stems. Put spinach in a large pot, sprinkle with a little salt and pepper, cover tightly, and cook with no added water over low heat for 8 to 10 minutes. Drain the cooked spinach in a colander and press out as much water as possible. Chop the spinach in the colander, letting it drain well. Peel onions and garlic.

Preheat oven to 350°F. Chop the ham, bacon, onion, garlic and fresh herbs. Sprinkle the mixture with the dried herbs. Mix all the chopped ingredients in a large bowl. Beat the eggs and mix them in. Break up the sausage meat and mix it in. Season the mixture, but use salt lightly since ham and sausage are both salty.

Use the lard to grease 2 oblong ovenproof dishes, 6-cup size, and line the dishes with slices of pork fatback; reserve some slices for the top. Put in the pâté mixture, pressing it down firmly, and smooth the top. Cover with reserved slices of fatback. Cover dishes securely with foil and stand them in a roasting pan. Pour in hot water to reach halfway up the baking dishes. Bake for 1 to 1¼ hours.

Remove dishes from oven and water bath; test that the pâtés are cooked. Remove the foil, take off the top layer of fat, and serve the pâtés hot. Or you may prefer to serve them cold; in that case, weight the pâtés, cool them, and chill them in the refrigerator. At serving time, remove the top layer of fat, turn out the pâtés, and slice.

Smoked Cod Roe Pâté

6 appetizer portions

3	large slices of white bread	1	tablespoon tomato juice
5	tablespoons melted butter		black pepper
6	ounces smoked cod roe		lemon wedges
2	teaspoons grated onion		black olives
3	ounces cream cheese		

Remove crusts from bread, tear slices into small bits, and soak in the butter for 5 minutes. Mix the cod roe with the grated onion in a bowl. Add the cheese and beat with a wooden spoon until thoroughly blended. Beat in the soaked bread and butter slowly, blending it in with a fork. Gradually mix in the tomato juice and season well with pepper to taste.

Beat until the mixture is light and pale in color. Pile on a chilled dish and garnish with lemon wedges and black olives. Serve as soon as ready.

If you make this ahead, use olive oil instead of butter as the texture will be better after refrigerating.

English Potted Pork

4 to 6 portions

4	tablespoons lard	1	teaspoon minced fresh
6	tablespoons clarified butter		sage
1	pound cold roast pork,		freshly ground black
	without bones		pepper
½	teaspoon grated onion		

Melt lard and butter, and let them cool to room temperature. Cut any skin and excess fat off the meat. Mince it twice. Put the meat in a large mortar with the onion, sage, and pepper to taste. Pound well until reduced to a paste. Or purée it in a food processor, in batches. Pound in the softened butter, little by little, until well mixed and smooth. Check the seasoning and add more if needed.

Turn the paste into four to six ½-cup pots. Tap pots twice on the countertop to release any air bubbles. Leave ½-inch headspace and smooth the surface of the paste. Wipe the rims of the pots clean. Cover the paste with the cooled melted lard. When lard is firm, pour in a second layer. When lard is solid, label the pots, cover with foil, and refrigerate. Use within 2 days. These cannot be stored long like the *rillettes,* since they are not baked for many hours.

Terrine of Duck

8 portions

12	ounces unsalted fresh pork fatback	2	hard-cooked eggs
1	duck, 6 pounds	2	garlic cloves
½	cup brandy	1	teaspoon salt
2	canned truffles	½	teaspoon black pepper
8	ounces lean veal, ground	4	tablespoons butter
1	pound lean pork, ground	4	ounces duck or chicken livers

Have your butcher cut the pork fatback into very thin slices; also have him grind the veal and pork if not available already ground. Quarter the duck with poultry shears. Set the liver aside for the recipe; if it weighs less than 4 ounces, add enough chicken livers to make that amount. (Other duck giblets can be set aside for another use, or frozen.) Remove all the skin and obvious fat from the duck and carefully cut the meat from the bones. (Bones can be frozen for future stock making.) Place the duck meat on a chopping board and cut it into thin strips. Place strips in a mixing bowl and pour in ¼ cup of the brandy. Pour the canning juices of the truffles into the bowl. Cut truffles into very thin slices and add to the duck. Set aside to marinate for 1 hour.

Preheat oven to 350°F. In a large mixing bowl combine the veal and pork. Peel and chop the eggs; peel garlic cloves and put through a press. Add both to the meats, along with salt, pepper and remaining brandy. Mix ingredients until thoroughly combined. Melt the butter in a small skillet over moderate heat. Add the livers and sauté, stirring and turning them, for 3 minutes. Chop the livers and add to the meats.

Use half of the slices of pork fat to line a 2-quart terrine.

Spread one third of the veal and pork mixture into the bottom. Cover with one third of the duck and truffles and spoon a little of the marinade over. Lay a thin layer of pork strips on top. Continue making layers in the same fashion, ending with a thin layer of fat strips. Cover terrine with foil and place it in a roasting pan. Pour in enough hot water to come halfway up the sides of the terrine. Set the pan in the center of the oven and bake for 1½ hours, until the mixture is shrinking away from the sides of the container.

Remove terrine from the water bath and pour off any excess liquid. Place a foil-covered cardboard over the mixture and weight it. Chill the terrine for at least 8 hours, or overnight.

Remove weights and covering. Remove terrine from refrigerator at least 2 hours before serving it. Serve as a luncheon main dish, with crusty French bread.

Note: A 6-pound duck may be hard to find. In that case, purchase two 4-pound ducks and weigh 3 pounds of boned meat for the terrine. Extra duck meat can be saved for another recipe.

Terrine of Pork Tenderloin

8 to 10 portions

1½	pounds lean veal	4	ounces fresh pork fatback
	pinch of ground ginger	8	ounces smoked bacon
	pinch of cayenne pepper	1	whole pork tenderloin, about 12 ounces
4	oranges	1¼	cups liquid aspic stock
¼	cup white wine		
1	tablespoon Cointreau liqueur		

Cut the veal into cubes and put in a mixing bowl with the spices. Grate the rind of 1 orange and extract the juice of 2 oranges. Add rind, juice, wine and Cointreau to the veal. Toss to mix, and marinate for 3 hours, in a cool place or in the refrigerator.

Preheat oven to 350°F. Mince the marinated veal, the fatback and bacon together, or put through a meat grinder. Add enough of the marinade to have a moist mixture. Put half of this mixture into a long 6-cup baking dish. Lay the pork fillet down the center, if necessary folding in the thin ends. Cover with remaining veal mixture. Cover dish with foil

and bake in a water bath in the oven for 2 to 2½ hours. Pâté is cooked when the juices run clear.

Remove pâté from the oven and place a foil-covered lid or cardboard on top. Weight it, and refrigerate for 8 hours, or overnight, to become firm and cool.

When pâté is firm and cold, remove it from the terrine. Scrape off the fat. Cut remaining oranges into thin slices and arrange slices over the top of the pâté. Let the aspic stock cool to the point of setting. Spoon it over the pâté and oranges, and let it chill until set. If necessary spoon a second layer over the pâté. Chill pâté for 1½ hours, until aspic is set.

Liver Pâté with Garlic and Anchovies

6 to 8 portions

1	pound lamb liver	6	tablespoons brandy
3	anchovy fillets	2	tablespoons tomato purée
1	medium-size onion	½	teaspoon salt
3	garlic cloves	½	teaspoon black pepper
1	teaspoon butter	½	teaspoon crumbled dried thyme
4	ounces lean ground beef	½	teaspoon grated nutmeg
2	tablespoons chopped fresh parsley	6	tablespoons fine dry bread crumbs

Chop the lamb liver into ½-inch pieces. Drain and chop anchovies. Peel and mince onion. Peel garlic cloves and put through a press. Use the butter to coat a 4-cup terrine or baking dish. Preheat oven to 375°F.

Place the liver, ground beef, anchovies, garlic, onion and parsley in a blender, or food processor fitted with the steel blade, and chop on and off until the mixture is smooth. Spoon the mixture into a large mixing bowl and add the brandy, tomato purée, salt, pepper, thyme and nutmeg. Beat with a wooden spoon until well blended. Add the bread crumbs and beat until smooth.

Spoon the mixture into the buttered terrine and cover with foil. Set the terrine in a roasting pan half-filled with hot water. Place the pan in the oven and bake for 1 to 1½ hours, until a skewer inserted in the center comes out clean. Remove pan from oven and lift terrine out of the water. Remove the foil cover and set the pâté aside to cool. When pâté is cool, place a heavy plate or other weight on top and refrigerate for at least 6 hours.

Serve the pâté from the terrine, or turn it out. Run a sharp knife around the edge to loosen the pâté; place an oval plate on top and invert plate and terrine together. Cut into slices and serve as part of a buffet meal or for a picnic.

Game Pâté

8 portions

1 pound boned game meat
(legs and wings of game
birds, portions of rabbit,
venison, etc.)
15 strips of smoked bacon
1 thick slice of bread
2 tablespoons milk
2 ounces mushrooms
2 tablespoons unsalted
butter

4 tablespoons salted butter
1 large egg
6 tablespoons medium-sweet
sherry
1 teaspoon grated orange
rind
salt and pepper
lard

Mince or shred the game and 5 bacon strips. Tear the bread into small pieces, put in a bowl, and pour the milk over it. Wipe the mushrooms, trim stems, and slice caps and stems. Melt the unsalted butter in a small pan and sauté the mushrooms until tender. Preheat oven to 350°F.

Squeeze the bread dry. Mix or pound together the meat, mushrooms and bread to the texture you choose—smooth paste or a coarser mixture with visible fragments of mushroom. Mix in the salted butter, egg, sherry and orange rind. Season generously.

Grease a 1-pound loaf pan or a baking dish of similar size with lard. Line with 7 of the remaining bacon strips. Fill the pan with the pâté mixture. Smooth the surface and cover

with remaining 3 bacon strips. Cover the pan tightly with foil. Stand in a roasting pan half-full of hot water. Bake for 1½ hours, until the meat shrinks slightly from the sides of the pan. Check with a skewer to be sure pâté is done.

Remove pâté from oven and water. Remove foil and top bacon strips. Spoon off any excess fat. Set the pan in a larger container of cold water. Cover pâté with foil-wrapped cardboard and add weights. Chill for 24 hours.

Remove cardboard and weights and refrigerate for another 24 hours. Turn out for serving. Serve as a first course with thin-sliced rye or pumpernickel bread, or serve as a main course for 4 portions.

Veal and Pork Pâté en Croûte

12 to 16 portions

2 batches of Flaky Pastry
(see Index)
1 pound fresh pork fatback
12 ounces fresh pork shoulder
12 ounces veal shoulder
8 ounces pork liver
4 tablespoons butter
1 tablespoon minced shallot
½ teaspoon minced garlic
12 ounces chicken livers
3 tablespoons brandy
2 large eggs

2 tablespoons heavy cream
2 teaspoons salt
½ teaspoon black pepper
¼ teaspoon ground coriander
¼ teaspoon ground allspice
¼ teaspoon grated nutmeg
pinch each of ground
cardamom, cinnamon
and cloves
butter and flour for mold
2 to 3 cups liquid aspic

Make the pastry, roll it into a ball, wrap with plastic wrap, and refrigerate for 2 hours.

Have the butcher cut the fatback into ⅛-inch-thick slices. Trim all sinews, gristle and bone from the pork, veal and liver. Cut meats into chunks and grind in a meat grinder or food processor. Put the mixture in a large bowl.

Melt 2 tablespoons butter in a skillet and sauté shallot and garlic until tender and beginning to color. With a slotted

spoon transfer both to the bowl of meats. Wash, dry, and trim the chicken livers. Melt remaining butter in the skillet and sauté livers, turning them to brown all sides, for about 6 minutes; livers should still be pink inside. Set livers aside. Deglaze the skillet with the brandy over high heat, scraping up any browned bits; pour the deglazing into the bowl of meats.

Preheat oven to 350°F. Beat 1 egg with the cream and

pour into the meats. Mix salt and all spices and sprinkle into the meats. (This mixture approximates French *sel épicé;* if you can find that, use 3 teaspoons of it instead.) Mix thoroughly. At this point the mixture can be pounded or processed to make it smoother, or it can remain as it is, somewhat rough-textured.

Remove pastry from refrigerator, let it rest at room temperature for 20 minutes, then roll it out to ¼-inch thickness. Use the top of a 2-quart hinged pâté mold or baking dish as a pattern to cut out a piece of pastry for the top; set the pastry lid aside, covered. Lightly butter and flour the mold and shake off any excess flour. Fit the pastry into the mold, using a lump of the dough to push it into place. Leave an extra piece of dough, about ½ inch, hanging over the edge of the mold all around.

Line the pastry with the slices of fatback, setting aside enough for the top. Press half of the ground mixture into the mold. Arrange the whole chicken livers on top in a pattern or in a line from one end to the other. Cover livers with remaining forcemeat and the forcemeat with remaining slices of fatback. Fold in the edge of the pastry all around.

Roll out the pastry for the lid to make it thinner. Moisten the folded pastry edge, and place the lid on top, sealing it to the moistened edge. Cut off extra pastry. Make a hole in the center for steam to escape; or, if your mold is oval or long, make 2 holes. Beat remaining egg with 1 tablespoon water and brush this egg wash all over the exposed pastry. If you like, you can cut out designs with the pastry scraps and glue them in place with more egg wash. Brush any decorations with more egg wash. Insert a funnel of foil in the steam vent.

Slide the pâté mold onto a baking sheet; a baking dish can go directly on the oven rack. Bake the pâté for 2 hours. If the crust seems to be browning too much, cover it with foil. The pâté is done when the fat rising in the funnel is completely clear.

Loosen the hinge of the mold and let the pâté cool to room temperature. Pour the liquid aspic into the pâté through the steam vents to fill all spaces that developed during baking. Remove the mold and chill the pâté in the refrigerator. Cut into slices to serve.

Rillettes de Porc
(French Potted Pork)

about 12 ounces, 4 to 6 portions

1 pound boned pork belly
8 ounces fresh pork fatback
½ garlic clove
1 bay leaf

salt and black pepper
½ teaspoon crumbled dried
    thyme

Have the pork boned by the butcher; it is not easy for a home cook to do it. Have the rind removed. Cut the meat into strips 1 inch long and ¼ inch wide. Cut the fatback into small cubes. Preheat oven to 275°F.

Put the meat and fat in a heavy oven pot. Peel and crush garlic and add to the mixture with the bay leaf. Season with salt and pepper. Add ¼ cup water to the pot to prevent meat sticking. Cover the pot and bake in the oven for 4 hours. Shake the pot from time to time to be sure the meat is not sticking.

Place a large sieve over a clean saucepan. Turn the contents of the pot into the sieve. Let all the melted fat drip into the saucepan. Discard the bay leaf. Press the meat gently to get out as much fat as possible. Using 2 forks, shred the

meat. While shredding, mix in the thyme. Check seasoning and adjust if necessary; *rillettes* should be well seasoned.

Press the meat into small pots that hold ½ to ¾ cup. Leave at least ½-inch headspace. Wipe the rims of the pots clean and let the mixture cool. If the fat has become solid, warm it over gentle heat until melted. Remove fat from heat and let it cool, but do not let it become solid. Wring out a double layer of cheesecloth in warm water and ladle the fat through the cheesecloth into a clean bowl. When the pots of meat are cold, cover them with a thin layer of clarified fat. Let that layer become firm, then add a second layer of fat. Cool, label and refrigerate. *Rillettes* will keep under refrigeration for 1 month.

Terrine of Fresh Haddock and Smoked Codfish

6 to 8 portions

1	pound smoked cod fillet juice of ½ lemon	⅔	cup soft white bread crumbs
2	tablespoons white wine	1	egg yolk
10	ounces fresh haddock fillet	2	tablespoons heavy cream
3	tablespoons unsalted butter	3	bay leaves

Skin the cod fillet and cut 6 ounces of it into finger-length strips. Soak them in the lemon juice and wine for 1 hour.

Skin the haddock fillet. Mince the haddock with remaining codfish. Melt 2 tablespoons of the butter and stir it into the fish. Add bread crumbs, egg yolk and cream. Pound the mixture to a smooth paste, or purée it in a food processor. Mix in all of the lemon juice and wine in which the cod strips soaked, to make a soft paste.

Preheat oven to 350°F. Use remaining tablespoon of butter to coat a 4-cup deep baking dish with a lid. Press in about half of the fish paste and cover with the codfish strips.

Press in remaining fish paste and smooth the top. Arrange bay leaves in a trefoil pattern on top. Cover the dish tightly with foil, then with the lid. Stand the dish in a pan of very hot water and bake for 40 to 45 minutes.

Remove dish from the oven and from the pan of water. Lift off lid and foil, and pour off any excess liquid on top of the pâté. Cover the pâté with foil-wrapped cardboard and weight it. Set the dish in a pan of cold water and chill for at least 12 hours. Remove weight and cardboard, cover with plastic wrap, and refrigerate. To serve, cut into slices in the dish. Accompany with salads and toast.

Part Two

QUICK FRYING POULTRY, MEAT AND FISH

Frying is the liveliest form of stovetop cookery. The sight of food sizzling briskly in hot butter or oil promises something short, sweet, and to the point, as suggested by the literal meaning of the French word *sauter,* to jump, the term used for quick cooking in little fat. This is the kind of cooking that kitchen minimalists—college students with hot plates, bachelors who can't boil water, weekend cottagers—most associate with basic survival. You are more likely to find a skillet than a stockpot or casserole in the kitchen of a busy person setting up housekeeping. Short-order cooking in restaurants is almost synonymous with frying, either simple sautéing in a shallow layer of butter or oil, or deep-frying in a surrounding bath of very hot fat. The advent in recent years of the Chinese technique of stir-frying, or tossing cut-up ingredients in oil over high heat for a few minutes, can only reinforce the association of the frying method with quickness and simplicity.

However, it should not be thought that the only virtue of frying is convenience. It does things for the flavors of food that other methods cannot duplicate.

Fat and oils—which are both fat except that oils are liquid and fats solid at room temperature—have an advantage over water in that they do not boil at 212°F. They thus make possible a modulation of cooking temperatures within a range intermediate between the gentle heat of poaching or steaming and the fiercer heat of the primeval fire-based methods like broiling and spit-roasting. They function in several ways at once: to lubricate the surface of the pan and prevent the food sticking as moisture evaporates; to interpose a layer of slightly cooler temperature between the food and the much hotter metal of the pan; and most tellingly, to form the actual medium in which the food cooks. Frying is the art of using fat as a cooking medium, and should be based on a respect for cooking fats and their qualities.

To understand the contribution of the fat used to fried foods, it is necessary to realize that the flavors you taste in a completed dish are not what you would get by simply adding up the ingredients that went into it—so much lemon juice, so much garlic, and so forth. There are elements of elusive flavor or virtually no flavor at all that seem to alter the way in which we perceive other flavors, and the most important of these are fats and oils. They seem to redefine the flavors of foods cooked in them. Imagine, if you will, Japanese *tempura* cooked in olive oil instead of soy oil, Middle Eastern eggplant fried in butter rather than olive oil, Alsatian sliced potatoes sautéed in peanut oil, not goose fat. In each case the contribution of the fat to the total effect is out of all proportion to what you might suppose from tasting it in isolation.

Part of the reason is that fats and oils tend to coat things instead of blending with them. Chemically insoluble in water or water-based liquids like stocks or juices, they form a kind of physical buffer between other foods and the taste-bud receptors, softening and diffusing the sharp individual flavors of things so that they seem to broaden or mingle. Cooking fats do not accept most flavors in the way that a kettle of water or broth would accept the flavor of vinegar or salt thrown into it, yet the particular flavors they do hold are astonishingly pervasive. The taste of badly fried food will stay with you for hours; properly fried food seems to release fragrance as you bite into it.

The use of these marvelous substances cannot be one of the oldest forms of cooking. The techniques of frying had to await the knowledge of how to extract oil from fruits or seeds, butter from milk, or fat from meat; this last also involved the ability to make vessels capable of withstanding the high temperatures necessary for rendering fat. All cuisines eventually developed some form of it, and all became firmly wedded to the use of their own preferred kind of cooking fat.

The first lesson to be learned in frying is to respect the authenticity of flavor that can be achieved only by a firsthand knowledge of butter, lard, oils, and different fats as they taste when used as they are used in the cooking of a particular region.

Around the Mediterranean, home of the olive tree, the accepted medium was olive oil, which varies immensely from region to region depending on the particular kind of olive or style of pressing. Much of northern Europe, favorably situated for raising cattle, adopted butter, which also varies greatly according to the favored breed of cow and the preference for butter churned from sour or sweet cream.

Pig-raising areas such as Hungary and many parts of Italy and central Europe took to lard. Rendered goose fat became a favorite cooking staple in Alsace, while the Eastern European Jews adopted rendered chicken fat. Where the cuisine of lamb was dominant, from the eastern Mediterranean into central Asia, a special breed of sheep was developed with huge deposits of tail fat. In India everyday cookery often used vegetable oils, but the most admired of cooking fats is ghee, butter made from buffalo milk, which takes on a nutty flavor from long, slow heating. The Far East is unique in its dislike of fragrant, flavorful fats as cooking mediums; animal fat is seldom used there; the preferred cooking oil in China and Japan is soy, completely tasteless and intended only as a background to the foods so artfully cooked in it. However, tiny amounts of other highly flavored oils are added to foods as aromatic flavorings.

In many parts of the world, panfrying and sautéing are considered refined culinary skills, worthy of being applied to the most superb dishes. Italy is one center of exquisite fried foods *(fritti)*, from first courses like *mozzarella in carrozza* (literally, "mozzarella in a carriage," mozzarella cheese sandwiched between bread slices, the whole thing dipped into egg and deep-fried) to desserts like batter-dipped pieces of fruit and "fried cream" *(crema fritta,* a very stiff, heavy pastry cream coated with egg and bread crumbs before frying). The majority of *fritti*, however, are fish, meat, chicken, sliced vegetables, and various kinds of croquettes.

Olive oil is used in some areas, but much of northern Italy prefers butter or vegetable oils, and lard is often used in the area around Rome. This can alter the effect of the finished dish, since butter cannot be heated to the same temperature as lard or most oils without becoming full of bitter blackened particles and thus cannot crisp a batter or breading as effectively as oils. Olive oil smokes at a slightly lower temperature than most other oils, but not enough to affect the crispness and browning of fried foods. In regions where butter is preferred, it is often clarified for frying, or mixed with a tasteless vegetable oil to preserve some butter flavor without the risk of burning.

In addition to *fritti,* the Italians have a high regard for sautéed veal, a meat whose delicate, quick-cooking texture is particularly suited to this cooking method. Italy is even responsible for a veal dish that has somehow switched national identities in the eyes of most diners. This is the Viennese cutlet, or *Wiener Schnitzel,* which crossed the Alps from Milan in the nineteenth century, when most of northern Italy was still part of the Hapsburg Empire.

A far odder and older transplant is *tempura,* which was unknown in Japan until the advent of Western missionaries in the sixteenth century. Both the word and the technique are apparently of Portuguese origin, though it is not known just what foods the visitors taught the islanders to fry in batter. Whatever the stimulus, it acted on the Japanese imagination to produce the world's most exquisitely delicate fried foods, categorically known as *agemono* (fried things). Compared to *tempura* most Western egg-and-crumb coatings seem heavy. Yet there are no secret ingredients in the batter. It is simply a thin, slightly lumpy paste of flour and water, sometimes with egg. When flour-dusted shrimps and vegetables are dipped into it, then quickly immersed in hot oil, the batter turns into an airy, crunchy coating that gives the lie to all who consider deep-fried foods indigestible.

The United States has its own candidates for distinction in the fried-food department, the most notable of which is Southern fried chicken. The most delicate versions of this dish are not deep-fried but panfried in a generous amount of fat and not breaded but simply dipped into seasoned flour. In the days of its glory the chicken was cooked in lard, clarified butter, or strained bacon or salt-pork drippings.

Stir-frying, the distinctive Chinese contribution to fat-based cookery, is also the quickest of frying techniques. The ingenious design of the wok enables a very small amount of hot oil to "surprise" (as the French say) a large quantity of ingredients—that is, rapidly to seal in the sharpness and distinctiveness of their individual flavors. The results unite something of the purity and freshness of taste and superior preservation of nutrients achieved by poaching or steaming with the rounder, richer effect of frying. What oil and cooking juices there are keep running to the bottom rather than evaporating over the whole surface, and when the food is tossed it slides back along the curve of the wok to keep being re-exposed to the oil and liquid at the bottom, so that it is continually re-coated and moistened.

Now, as never before, with so many ethnic cuisines available to us, the practice of proper frying and sautéing deserves to be valued for its ability to make flavors blossom into richness and completeness.

QUICK FRYING

Methods of quick frying, be they called sauté, stir-fry, panfry or quick-braise, are classic in almost every cuisine for producing exceptionally good meals. Sautéing is probably the most frequently used technique in fine French restaurants, where meals are cooked individually, while the Chinese use stir-frying as their primary cooking method.

Frying methods require high-quality ingredients; meat, poultry and fish need to be tender and vegetables must be fresh. Butter and oils should be fresh and chosen for their unique qualities of taste. Whichever method you use, you can be confident if you follow the procedures listed here and pay careful attention when:

- selecting suitable cuts of meat
- preparing the meat
- choosing the correct methods of frying
- controlling the cooking temperature and time.

All methods of frying require fairly high heat to seal foods and allow them both to cook and to remain moist and tender. Careful control of temperature is a vital factor in successful frying. After the initial sealing and browning, the method of cooking will vary according to the type of food you are preparing.

Fish, poultry and meats can be cooked in fat, usually butter, oil, or a combination of both, in various ways, giving quick, flavorful results. While frying is considered a dry-heat procedure, there are some variations that begin by quickly frying the food to seal the surface and continue with added moisture, becoming a sort of braising.

Sautéing Fish

Good fish for sautéing include fillets and steaks, no thicker than 1 inch; scallops or cutlets made from larger fish; small whole fish such as small trout, smelts, small herring. If you have very thin fillets such as 2- to 4-ounce pieces of flounder, cook them directly in the chosen fat, without any sort of coating. These little pieces of fish will cook in 2 or 3 minutes, faster than any coating; if you coat them, the fish will be done and the coating still raw. Fillets or steaks 1 inch thick will be improved with some sort of coating, as it will keep the outside from overcooking while the center is getting done. Small whole fish can be coated or not depending on their thickness.

Foods that are cooked over high heat or for a longer time need a fat that does not break down or smoke. Since fish cooks so quickly, the fat to use can be clarified butter, or a mixture of oil and raw butter, or oil alone.

Set a sauté pan or flat, heavy skillet over high heat and add enough butter and/or oil to coat the bottom with a very thin layer. When a drop of water will skip across the pan, adjust the heat; the pan must not be too hot for uncoated foods, and especially not for fish. Add the pieces of fish; sauté for 2 minutes, until golden, then flip them over with a pancake turner and cook on the other side for 1 to 1½ minutes, until golden on both sides. Do not delay in turning, as even ½ minute too long will soften the fish so that it is no longer easy to turn without breaking. Also, turn the thin pieces only once. Do not season until golden brown.

Thicker fillets, steaks and small whole fish, which need a few more minutes to be cooked through, can be helped by the addition of a coating, which serves to protect the outside while the inside is being finished. The most used coating is flour, which is known as *à la meunière,* or "in the style of the miller's wife." It is simply coating fish with seasoned flour, sautéing it in clarified butter, and serving it with more butter, lemon juice and parsley.

Fish à la Meunière

4 portions

8 flounder fillets, about 4 ounces each
4 tablespoons seasoned flour
4 tablespoons clarified butter
4 teaspoons lemon juice
2 tablespoons chopped fresh parsley

- Frying frozen fish. Commercially frozen fish products usually carry full instructions and cooking times on the package. Frozen fish is best cooked from the near frozen state, preferably within 30 minutes of being taken from the freezer. It is best cooked coated, making it perfect for *meunière* treatment, and the slight softening of the surface as the fish defrosts helps the flour to stick more firmly.
- Cook the fish in exactly the same way as fresh fish, allowing half of the cooking time on each side.

5 Arrange the cooked fillets overlapping on a hot dish. Keep them hot.

1 Divide the fillets along the center seam to make 16 small strips. Rinse and pat dry.

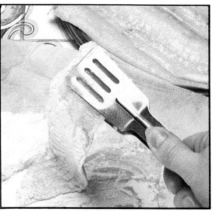

2 Spread seasoned flour on a sheet of wax paper. Press fillets into flour and shake off excess.

3 Heat half of the clarified butter in a large skillet. Sauté half of the quarter fillets for 3 to 4 minutes, until golden on both sides.

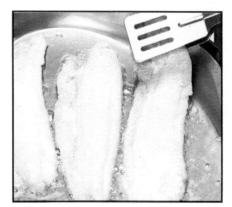

4 Add remaining fillets, and sauté until golden on both sides. This can be done in several batches if the pan is small.

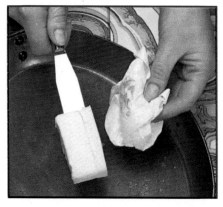

6 Wipe out the skillet and in it heat remaining butter until golden brown: watch carefully to keep the butter from burning.

7 Pour brown butter over the fish, then sprinkle with the lemon juice and parsley. Serve at once.

Sautéed fish is enhanced by the sharp contrast of piquant flavors. Not without reason, lemon juice is the classic companion of fried fish. For a change, try lime juice or orange juice. Sauces should be well flavored and spicy or piquant. They can be hot such as Almond and Walnut Sauce (see Index), or cold such as mayonnaise.

Vegetables are often served with sautéed fish almost as part of the dish, to add color and succulence. The vegetables are cooked briefly after the fish has been prepared and coated, but before it is cooked. In this way, the vegetables are ready to serve as soon as the fish is cooked. Once cooked, they are kept warm while the fish is being sautéed and are spooned over the fish just before serving. The vegetables that are most suitable are moist varieties, such as tomatoes, onions, mushrooms, cucumbers, celery and leeks.

Sautéing Poultry

Among chefs, sautéing is a favorite way of cooking poultry. In his *Guide to Modern Cookery*, Escoffier gives no less than 44 different ways to present sautéed chicken. Any type of poultry is suitable for sautéing provided it is young and tender, but at the same time plump and meaty.

Poultry and meats, being thicker and less fragile than fish, can be cooked at higher heat. However, thin lean pieces such as slices of chicken breast and veal scallops need just as much care as thin fish. A thin coating prevents the escape of meat juices.

Good poultry for sautéing includes chicken breasts, split down the breastbone, each half used if they are small, or the breasts divided or cut into thin scallops. Scallops can be made from turkey breast, legs and thighs.

Sautéing Meat

The best meat choices for sautéing include the veal scallop (*escalopes* in French, *scaloppini* in Italian), cut from the round of the leg or shoulder; pork scallops can be made

Cutting Veal Scallops

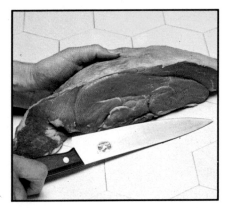

1 Wipe the veal round (leg) with a damp cloth. Put it on a cutting board.

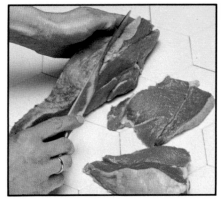

2 With a sharp knife cut diagonal slices from the meat.

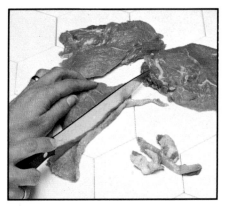

3 Remove all skin, membrane, fat and any bits of gristle from all the slices.

4 Place each scallop between 2 sheets of wax paper or plastic wrap.

5 Beat with a rolling pin or the flat side of a cleaver to flatten to 1/8-inch thickness.

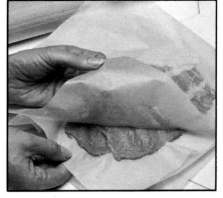

6 Scallops are ready to use. If you plan to use them later, store in wax paper, or plastic wrap.

Cutting Chicken Scallops

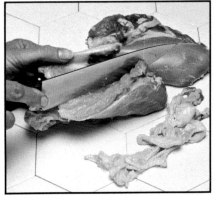

1 Peel the skin from the breast, split it in half, then cut down with a sharp knife between the flesh and ribs to remove bones.

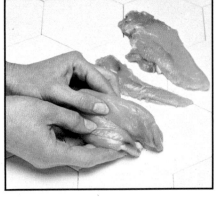

2 Divide each breast half into two with your fingers. The flesh separates naturally, giving 2 fillets, one smaller than the other.

3 Flatten the fillets between 2 sheets of wax paper to 1/3-inch thickness. Chicken does not flatten as easily as veal.

Fresh Bread Crumbs

1 *Food processor method:* With steel blade in place, add cubes of firm bread to work bowl.

2 Pulsate on/off for 5 seconds. Crumbs should be fine and even-sized; avoid overprocessing.

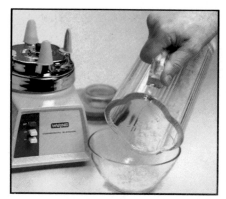

1 *Blender method:* Place firm bread cubes in blender container. Grate for 15 seconds, or until crumbs are as small as desired.

from the leg or the loin, and beef scallops from top round or top sirloin. These can be flattened into ¼-inch-thick layers. Slices of calf's liver and beef liver are also good sautéed.

Unlike veal scallops, pork scallops are not part of the classic cuisine tradition, but are a relatively new idea for cooking pork; these pieces can be treated much the same as veal. Pork tenderloin is solid meat with very little waste. When cut into scallops and flattened, it goes quite a long way. Buy the weight of meat that you will actually serve. Allow 4 ounces per person, plus 1 to 2 ounces for trimmings. Cut and flatten the scallops in the same way as the veal scallops, to a thickness of not more than ¼ inch.

Another excellent choice for sautéing is a slice of boneless beef, such as tournedos, the thin slices of the beef filet, or the *médaillons* cut from these slices, or the *petit filets* from the thinnest end of the filet. Similarly *noisettes,* the boneless center meat of a lamb, pork or veal chop, are good for sautéing. These meats are all tender and relatively lean, so the small amount of butter, fat or oil used in sautéing is necessary to keep them from drying.

Sautéing Preparation

Clarified butter is the best fat for chicken, oil is good for meats, but use either if it suits your recipe better or if you have a particular preference.

These days there is a great variety of oils to choose from—fruity olive oils, pungent sesame oil (to be used only in very small amounts for flavoring), light oils, heavy ones and everything in between.

Meunière coating can be used for fish and some other sautéed meats, but in addition crumbs, egg and crumbs, rolled oats, cornmeal, ground nuts, matzo meal, egg white and cornstarch can be used. When using a combination of egg and crumbs, remember that this coating is useful only if the food needs at least 5 minutes of cooking for each side.

Bread Crumbs. Crumbs made of various kinds of bread are one of the most useful toppings and garnishes in the home kitchen. While one can buy dried bread crumbs in every supermarket, fresh crumbs need to be made at home. Use any firm bread—white, French, whole-wheat, rye, or whatever you prefer. Each kind of bread makes crumbs with its own special flavor. The

most useful are crumbs made from French bread or homemade white bread. Use fresh bread for fresh crumbs. Completely trim off all crusts.

If you have a food processor, tear the slices into small pieces and drop them into the bowl fitted with the steel blade. Process about 1 cup of pieces at a time. A single slice of standard white bread will make about ¾ cup of soft fresh crumbs. If you will not be using all of the crumbs at once, freeze them in airtight freezer bags. They will keep for at least 6 weeks. If you lack a food processor, use a hand grater and carefully rub the whole slice of bread against the side with coarse holes.

To prepare fish, poultry or meat for sautéing, trim the slices, remove membranes, and flatten if the piece requires it. Rinse fish and pat dry. Wipe poultry and meat with a damp paper towel. Add coating, if using one. Pour the fat into the pan, heat it, and put pieces in the pan in a single layer, with a little space between them. Do not overlap them, do not crowd the pan, and do not cover the pan. The food should not steam; the outside, whether coated or not, should quickly become crisp. Season each side only after sautéing. If you have too many pieces to fit in the pan,

Coating Meat with Egg and Crumbs

1 Have ready the pieces of meat, an egg, seasoned flour, and dried or fresh bread crumbs.

2 Break the egg into a shallow bowl, add 1 tablespoon water, and beat with a fork.

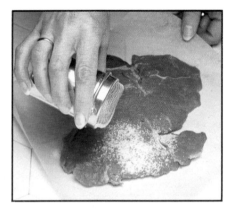

3 Pat meat dry with paper towels; lay pieces on wax paper. Sprinkle with seasoned flour. Or shake meat in a bag of seasoned flour.

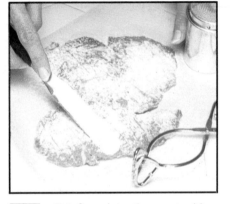

4 Pat flour into the meat with a spatula, then lift each piece with tongs and gently shake off excess flour.

5 Dip the meat, piece by piece, into the beaten egg; drain briefly. Place meat on bread crumbs, spread out on sheet of wax paper.

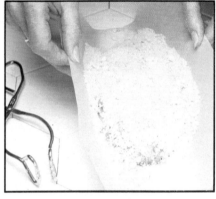

6 Lift the edges of the paper to coat the other side of the meat.

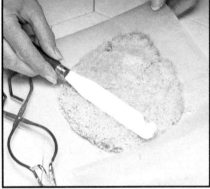

7 Transfer crumb-coated pieces to a clean sheet of wax paper and press gently with a spatula on both sides.

8 Let coated meat rest in a cool place, loosely covered with wax paper, for about 30 minutes. Do not refrigerate.

9 Sift remaining bread crumbs. Remove damp crumbs and reserve dry crumbs for future use.

sauté them in several batches. The amount of fat used in sautéing is so small that usually the food needs no draining.

Deglazing the pan is another important characteristic of a true sauté dish, which usually requires a sauce.

After the meat is cooked, remove it and pour away excess fat, if any, leaving about 1 tablespoon in the pan. Add the liquid stated in the recipe, which may be red or white wine, a well-flavored stock, dry white vermouth, mushroom cooking liquid or something similar. Boil rapidly to reduce and concentrate the liquid, at the same time stirring to dissolve and incorporate the browned juices from the bottom of the pan. In some recipes the sauce is completed by thickening and enriching this small amount of liquid with pieces of butter or with thick cream. In others, a well-flavored, previously prepared and thickened sauce is added.

Stir-Frying

This is a special kind of sautéing. Fish, poultry and meats are cut into small strips or cubes. Very little oil is used in a wok or skillet. The pieces are continuously stirred over brisk heat so that all sides are evenly browned.

If you are cooking a dish of several ingredients, usually the flavoring ingredients are cooked first—garlic, gingerroot—then the principal ingredient. The pieces of meat or fish are removed from the wok and put aside. The wok is wiped out, a little more oil is poured in, and the vegetables are stir-fried. Fish or meat pieces are returned to the pan, liquids are poured in, and everything is cooked together over high heat until tender. The liquid should be reduced to a few tablespoons of moist sauce.

Preparing Chicken for Stir-Frying

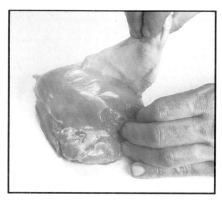

1 Start with chicken breasts that have been halved and deboned. Using fingers, pull skin off breast.

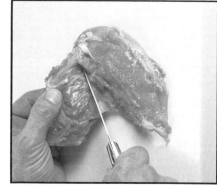

2 Place each half breast on cutting board and remove any ribs or bits of cartilage that may still be attached.

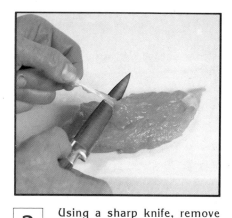

3 Using a sharp knife, remove white tendon.

4 To slice, hold blade horizontally with cutting edge parallel to meat grain. With sawing motion, cut slices about ⅛ inch thick.

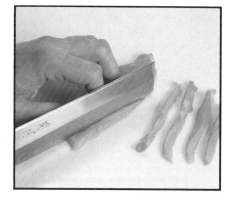

5 Stack slices with grain running lengthwise, and cut straight down along the grain to make even-size shreds.

6 Prepare coating mixture, if using. Work into slices with fingers. Chill for 30 minutes. Return to room temperature before cooking.

Stir-Frying Method

1 Have all ingredients ready. Heat oil in the wok and stir-fry garlic and gingerroot for 20 seconds.

2 Add the ingredients in order of cooking time required—in this case, shrimps first. Stir-fry for 2 to 3 minutes. Remove from wok.

3 Add next ingredient—here it is snow peas. Toss gently, so that small amount of oil coats vegetable. Stir-fry for 2 minutes.

Panfrying Meat

4 portions

4 beef steaks, each 6 to 8 ounces, about 1 inch thick
4 tablespoons unsalted butter
2 tablespoons oil
freshly ground black pepper
salt

• Use any tender cut of beef such as club steak, slices of the tenderloin, shell steaks, or pieces of sirloin.
• Pour melted butter flavored with parsley, tarragon, mustard, shallots or garlic over the steaks when ready to serve.
• Have garnishes such as tomatoes, parsley and watercress, and accompanying side dishes, ready before you cook the steaks, so that the meat can be served immediately.

3 Before the butter begins to brown, put in the steaks, one at a time. Raise the heat to sear the meat.

4 Panfry over brisk heat for about 6 minutes on one side. Use tongs to turn steaks.

5 Panfry second side in the same fashion. It may take less time to cook the second side. Nick meat with a knife to test.

Shallow Frying or Panfrying

4 Return shrimps to the wok, along with the snow peas.

5 Add glaze, if desired. All ingredients should be coated and heated, but avoid overcooking. Serve immediately.

1 Wipe steaks with a damp paper towel, trim excess fat, and nick edges to prevent buckling in the pan. Pat dry carefully.

2 Heat butter and oil in a heavy skillet over moderate heat. Sprinkle pepper into the melted butter.

6 Lift steaks with tongs and let excess fat drip into the pan. There will be very little fat.

7 Transfer steaks to a warm platter. Season with salt and additional pepper if you like. Garnish.

This process is used for thicker pieces of meat and poultry that need longer cooking. More fat is used. The pan for this must be very sturdy. Cast iron, cast aluminum or enameled cast iron are the best choices.

Chops of all kinds, chicken parts, rolled and stuffed scallops, hamburgers and other chopped mixtures are good cooked this way. Some of these can be cooked with or without a coating. Croquettes, fish balls or meat cakes other than hamburgers need a coating to give them greater stability. Thick pieces of fish can be panfried; these too need a coating. Egg and crumbs make the ideal coating for all panfried foods.

Panfried foods should be cooked according to specific recipe timing instructions. The timing is related to the thickness of the cut, and whether the meat is required to be rare, medium rare or well done.

It is important that the meat be of an even thickness throughout, and cut across the grain to encourage tenderness. If the meat is cut thinner than 1 inch the time needed is less.

When the food is done, it should be transferred from the pan to a warmed serving platter. If it is left in the pan, moisture will accumulate and make the coating soggy.

One of the benefits of this method is that you are left with meaty juices in the pan. With very little effort these can be made into a delicious sauce or gravy to pour over the meat.

If there is more than 1 tablespoon of fat remaining in the pan, pour it off. Replace with 2 tablespoons fresh butter.

Add ½ cup good stock, consommé, red wine, dry white wine or dry vermouth to the pan and place over high heat. Stir and scrape the meat juices from the bottom of the pan and boil until the liquid is reduced to about 3 tablespoons and is of a syrupy consistency. Spoon the sauce over the meat and serve immediately. For a more refined sauce, this deglazing can be strained.

Veal Sauté Chasseur

4 portions

12 small veal scallops, each 2
    ounces
5 tablespoons unsalted butter
3 tablespoons oil
4 shallots
1 small garlic clove
1 pound tomatoes
6 ounces mushrooms
¼ teaspoon dried marjoram
    or tarragon
    salt and black pepper
2 teaspoons cornstarch
½ cup beef stock
½ cup dry white wine

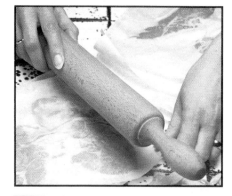

1 Remove all skin, fat and tissue surrounding the scallops. Beat to flatten and pat dry.

2 Heat 2 tablespoons of the butter and 1 tablespoon oil in a large sauté pan over medium heat.

6 Peel and crush garlic; peel, seed, and chop tomatoes; wipe and slice mushrooms.

10 Add a little hot sauce to cornstarch, then stir this into the sauce. Boil, uncovered, for 3 to 5 minutes.

3 When foam subsides add 3 or 4 scallops; do not crowd the pan. Sauté for 3 to 4 minutes.

4 Turn scallops and sauté until juices run clear when pierced with a knife. Remove and keep warm.

5 Sauté remaining scallops, adding butter and oil as necessary. Reserve. Peel and chop shallots.

7 Check that the pan contains at least 2 tablespoons fat. Add shallots and sauté for a minute or two.

8 Add tomatoes, garlic, herbs and seasoning to the pan. Cover and simmer for several minutes.

9 Blend cornstarch with 1 tablespoon stock. Add remaining stock and wine to pan and heat.

11 Melt 1 teaspoon butter with 2 teaspoons oil in a small pan. Sauté the mushrooms until soft.

12 Add mushrooms to sauce, reduce heat, and simmer for 1 minute. Taste and adjust seasoning.

13 Season scallops lightly with salt and pepper. Return to pan, cover and heat gently, without boiling, for 2 to 3 minutes.

Pan-Broiling

Pan-broiling is different from sautéing and panfrying since it uses no fat, or at most a few drops brushed on the pan. A pan for broiling must be heavy and sturdy, also perfectly even; a ridged pan is particularly good since it allows any fat in the meat to drain off. The heat used for pan-broiling is hotter than that used for sautéing or panfrying, and the pan is heated to the appropriate temperature before the meat is put in it. The meat is quickly seared so the outside is browned while the inside is rare. The cooking time is short. The meat used should be at least 1 inch thick; thin pieces would dry out in this method. Meat is the food most often pan-broiled; fish and chicken are not well suited to this method.

Quick-Braising

Quick-braising is one of the most-used processes in the home kitchen, although most people never think to give it a title. In classic cookery it is still called "sautéing." The food is first sautéed or panfried, then finished in a liquid. This process is seldom used for fish, since its natural tenderness does not require the extra cooking, but it is a good method for chicken quarters, or legs of larger birds, thick chops and cutlets, and for any piece of meat from a less tender cut such as top round or chuck, or pieces not from prime cuts but from choice or good grades, which will be flavorful but may be tough.

In quick-braising a moist, steam-filled atmosphere is created once the lid is placed over the pan. In this humid atmosphere, it is impossible for the meat to dry out—even pork, which often needs longer cooking.

Another feature of this method is that everything in the pan becomes part of the finished dish, so be sure to trim the poultry or meat well, removing skin, membranes, any external fat. Wipe the meat with a moistened paper towel. If necessary, scrape meat to remove any crumbs of bone or fat. Pat meat dry. Use a sauté pan or skillet with a tight-fitting lid.

Heat the oil or fat in the pan. Do not coat the meat. Place the pieces in the pan in a single layer. Sauté on both sides; the heat should be brisk but not so hot that the fat burns. When both sides are browned, add vegetables (tender types are best) for flavor, texture and moisture. These should be already prepared. Add vegetables to the pan and stir them in the fat until they begin to cook. If these vegetables will add enough moisture, cover the pan tightly and steam everything until the meat is tender. If not, add a few tablespoons of water or appropriate stock.

If you have meat that needs longer cooking, add liquid in addition to the vegetables. Let vegetables cook for about 5 minutes, then add the chosen liquid, which should be at room temperature or warmed. Wine, vermouth, cider, soy sauce, condiment sauces, tomato and other vegetable juices are possible choices. For some special dishes sweet cream or sour cream adds the perfect finish. Cream is usually added at the end, just long enough to be heated and mixed with the rest of the ingredients; long cooking causes cream to separate. A typical example of a dish finished with sour cream is Beef Stroganoff. The quick-braising method is necessary for this dish if you use any beef cut other than slices of the filet.

Beef Stroganoff

6 portions

1½	pounds top round of beef		1	tablespoon flour
	freshly ground black pepper		1	tablespoon tomato purée
			½	teaspoon Dijon-style mustard
2	medium-size onions		1	cup beef stock
6	ounces button mushroom caps		½	cup dairy sour cream
				chopped parsley
4	tablespoons unsalted butter		3	cups cooked rice

Have the beef cut into ½-inch-thick slices. Cut away and discard any fat or skin. Lay the slices on a board and flatten them with a wooden mallet, a cleaver or a rolling pin. Cut slices into ¼-inch-wide strips and the strips into 1-inch lengths. Sprinkle with pepper and rub it in lightly. Peel onions and cut into thin slices. Wipe mushroom caps with a damp cloth and cut them into thin slices.

When ready to cook, melt the butter in a wide sauté pan over low heat. Add onions and cook them gently for 5 minutes. Add mushrooms and continue cooking for another 3 to 4 minutes, stirring from time to time. Add the meat strips, increase heat to moderate, and sauté, stirring frequently, for about 5 minutes. Sprinkle in the flour, stir, and sauté for another minute. Stir the tomato purée and the mustard into the stock and add to the pan, stirring to mix in smoothly. Bring to a simmer, cover tightly, and simmer for 30 to 35 minutes, until the meat is very tender. Check the seasoning, stir in the sour cream, and heat gently without boiling.

Arrange cooked rice in a shallow serving bowl, ladle the beef over the rice, garnish with parsley, and serve immediately.

Steak au Poivre
(Steak with Peppercorns)

6 portions

6 beef shell steaks, 2 to 2½
   pounds altogether, cut
   about ¾ inch thick
2 tablespoons mixed black
   and white peppercorns

3 tablespoons olive oil
5 tablespoons unsalted
   butter
salt
juice of ½ lemon

Wipe the steaks with a damp cloth and nick the edges at ½-inch intervals. Crush the peppercorns in a mortar with a pestle. Spread the crushed peppers out on a flat board. Press first one side of each steak into the crushed peppercorns, then the other, pressing the beef down firmly to make the peppercorns stick to thé meat. Sprinkle the steaks lightly with 2 tablespoons olive oil, cover with a piece of wax paper, and leave in a cool place for 30 minutes to 2 hours.

When ready to cook, heat 3 tablespoons of the butter and remaining oil in a large skillet. Sauté the steaks in a single layer for about 3 minutes on each side for medium rare, longer for well done. Do them in several batches, as necessary. Adjust the heat to maintain an even temperature throughout the cooking time, but do not let the fat burn. Transfer the steaks to a hot serving dish and sprinkle with salt.

Pour the fat and peppercorns out of the skillet. Put remaining butter in the skillet and heat over moderate heat while scraping up the browned juices from the pan with a wooden spoon. Add the lemon juice, stir, and pour the deglazing over the steaks. Serve immediately.

Variation: After taking the steaks out of the pan, pour off the cooking fat and peppercorns and pour in ½ cup dry white wine, dry white vermouth or robust red wine. Boil briskly until reduced to 3 or 4 tablespoons, stirring to release the browned juices from the bottom of the pan. Off the heat stir in 2 tablespoons butter in small pieces, letting each piece emulsify before adding another. Spoon the pan sauce over the steaks.

Club Steaks with Mushrooms

2 portions

2 club or minute steaks,
 each 6 ounces
8 ounces button mushrooms
1 large garlic clove (optional)
 freshly ground black
 pepper

1 tablespoon oil
4 tablespoons butter
 salt
 juice of ½ lemon
1 tablespoon chopped fresh
 parsley or snipped chives

Wipe the steaks with a damp cloth, trim off excess fat, and dry on both sides with paper towels. Wipe mushrooms and trim base of stems. Cut caps and stems into thin slices. Peel garlic clove, if you use it, halve it, and rub the cut halves liberally over both sides of the steaks. Season with black pepper.

Put the oil and 2 tablespoons of the butter in a heavy skillet. Place over moderate heat until butter is melted and hot. Put in the steaks and sauté over brisk heat for about 2 minutes on each side, or a little longer if you prefer steak well done. Lift out steaks, holding them over the skillet to drain for a few seconds, then arrange on a hot serving dish and season with salt. Keep hot.

Melt remaining butter in the skillet and put in the mushrooms. Reduce the heat and cook gently, stirring often, until mushrooms soften and release their juices. Increase heat, season mushrooms with salt, and pour the lemon juice into the pan. Cook briskly over high heat, stirring, for 2 minutes, until most of the moisture has evaporated. Spoon mushrooms over the steaks and sprinkle with parsley or chives. Serve immediately.

Steaks with Red-Wine Sauce

4 portions

4 beef steaks, each 6 to 8
 ounces, 1 inch thick
4 tablespoons unsalted
 butter

1 tablespoon oil
 salt and pepper
2 shallots
½ cup red wine

Prepare the steaks for sautéing, remembering to nick the edges. Melt 2 tablespoons of the butter with the oil in a large skillet over moderate heat. When butter stops foaming, raise the heat and place the steaks in the pan. Sauté steaks until done to your liking. Remove pan from heat, season the steaks with salt and pepper on both sides, and transfer to a hot serving dish.

Peel and chop the shallots. Discard cooking fat and replace with 1 tablespoon of the butter. Melt butter over low heat and stir in chopped shallots. Cook slowly for 2 minutes. Pour in the wine, raise the heat, and boil rapidly, scraping up the meat juices from the bottom of the pan, until liquid has reduced to about 5 tablespoons.

Remove pan from heat and beat in remaining butter, in pieces, letting each piece emulsify before adding the next, until sauce is thickened. Season to taste and spoon over the steaks.

Variation: For steak *à la Bercy,* substitute dry white wine or dry vermouth for the red wine and stir in 2 tablespoons chopped fresh parsley before spooning the sauce over the steaks.

Pork Scallops with Apple and Lemon

4 portions

2 pork tenderloins, each 12
 ounces
 seasoned flour
1 large egg
¾ cup dry white bread
 crumbs

2 large cooking apples
 salt
5 tablespoons unsalted butter
2 tablespoons oil
1 lemon
 watercress

Cut the tenderloins into slices and flatten them as described for veal scallops. Coat each scallop with seasoned flour, beaten egg mixed with 1 tablespoon water, and bread crumbs. Leave scallops for 30 minutes to allow the coating to become firm.

Peel and core apples and cut each into six ¼-inch-thick rings. Drop into salted water, scant 1 tablespoon salt per 2 cups water, to prevent discoloration. Heat 2 tablespoons of the butter and the oil in a heavy frying pan. Sauté half of the scallops gently for 4 to 5 minutes on each side, until golden and cooked through. Lift out, drain on paper towels, and keep warm while sautéing the rest. Use a little extra butter if

necessary, reserving 2 tablespoons for cooking the apple rings.

Drain the apple rings, pat dry with paper towels, and dust lightly with seasoned flour, shaking off any excess. When all the scallops are cooked, pile them in the center of a serving platter and keep warm. Add remaining butter to the pan and sauté the apple rings in a single layer, until golden. Turn carefully, one at a time, and sauté on the other side. Lift out the apple rings and arrange them around the pork slices.

Squeeze the lemon and add the juice to the fat remaining in the pan. Heat while stirring to scrape up the browned juices, and pour this deglazing over the pork. Serve immediately, garnished with watercress.

Lamb Chops with Orange and Lemon

4 portions

8	rib or loin lamb chops	2	tablespoons drained capers
2	garlic cloves	½	cup orange juice
5	tablespoons olive oil		juice of 1 lemon
	salt and black pepper		lemon wedges
1	tablespoon minced fresh marjoram		

Prepare chops for sautéing; trim them and nick the edges. Peel and crush garlic cloves. Prepare a marinade by combining 3 tablespoons of the oil, the crushed garlic and a sprinkling of salt and pepper in a shallow glass or ceramic dish that will hold the chops in a single layer. Arrange chops in the dish and turn them or baste them to coat both sides with marinade. Cover loosely and refrigerate for 1 to 2 hours.

When ready to cook, lift chops from the marinade, scrape garlic back into the marinade, and pat chops dry with paper towels. Heat remaining oil in a large skillet. When hot,

sauté the chops over high heat until lightly browned, 2 to 3 minutes on each side. Pour off most of the fat in the skillet. Lower the heat; add the marinade, marjoram, capers and orange juice. Cover the pan and cook gently for 6 to 8 minutes, turning the chops once. Add the lemon juice to the pan and cook for a minute longer.

Arrange the chops on a large serving dish around a pile of sautéed potatoes. Spoon the pan juices over the chops and garnish with lemon wedges.

Lamb Chops with Mushrooms and Tomato Sauce

4 portions

1	onion		1	bay leaf
1	garlic clove		½	teaspoon salt
1	pound fresh tomatoes, or 1¾ cups canned tomatoes		½	teaspoon black pepper
2	tablespoons olive oil		2	tablespoons tomato paste
2	teaspoons minced fresh basil, or ½ teaspoon dried		8	slices of bread
			8	large mushroom caps
			4	tablespoons butter
			8	rib lamb chops, boned
			½	cup dry white wine

Peel and mince the onion; peel garlic and put through a press into the onion. Blanch and peel the tomatoes, and chop them. (If using canned tomatoes, chop them.) Heat the oil in a large saucepan over moderate heat. When hot, add the onion and garlic. Cook, stirring occasionally, for 5 to 7 minutes, until onion is soft and translucent but not brown. Add the tomatoes. (If you are using canned tomatoes, add the can juices too.) Add basil, bay leaf, salt, pepper and tomato paste. Reduce heat to low and simmer, stirring occasionally, for 30 minutes, adding a little water if the tomato sauce becomes too thick.

With a 3-inch cutter, cut rounds from the bread slices. Toast them, and arrange on a serving dish; keep the toast warm.

Wipe mushroom caps with a damp cloth. Melt 2 tablespoons butter in a large skillet over moderate heat. Add the mushrooms and sauté them, stirring occasionally, for 3 to 4 minutes, until they are tender. Drain mushrooms on paper towels, set aside, and keep warm. Add remaining butter to the pan and put in the boned chops, in a single layer. Sauté them for 4 to 6 minutes on each side, until they are tender but still slightly pink inside. Lift the lamb pieces from the pan and place them on the toast slices. Top each chop with a mushroom. Keep warm.

Add the wine to the skillet and stir well, scraping up the brown bits from the bottom of the pan with a wooden spoon. Increase heat to high and boil until wine is reduced by half. Stir in the tomato sauce, reduce heat to moderate, and cook for 5 minutes longer, stirring occasionally. Remove and discard the bay leaf. Spoon a little sauce over each chop and serve the rest separately.

Wiener Schnitzel

(Viennese Veal Scallops)

4 portions

8	veal scallops, each 3 ounces		6	tablespoons unsalted butter
	seasoned flour		2	tablespoons oil
½	cup dry white bread crumbs		8	pimiento-stuffed green olives
3	large eggs		4	tablespoons chopped fresh parsley
8	anchovy fillets		2	tablespoons capers (optional)
1½	lemons			

Prepare and flatten the veal scallops. Dust them lightly with the seasoned flour and shake off any excess. Pile the bread crumbs on a sheet of wax paper. Break 1 egg into a shallow bowl, add 1 tablespoon cold water, and beat with a fork to mix. Dip each scallop into the beaten egg and brush the egg all over it; lift out the meat and drain it briefly. Then dip each scallop into the bread crumbs, coating them thoroughly all over. Lay scallops on a flat surface and press the coating in place with a spatula. Cover lightly and leave for 30 minutes for the coating to set.

Meanwhile, prepare the garnishes. Hard-cook remaining 2 eggs, cool rapidly, shell them, and separate whites from yolks. Chop whites and press yolks through a fine sieve; keep separate. Roll up the anchovy fillets and cut 8 thin slices from one of the lemons.

When ready to sauté, heat 2 tablespoons of the butter

and the oil in a large skillet. Add as many scallops as will fit in the pan in a single layer. Sauté over moderate heat for 3 to 5 minutes on each side, depending on thickness. Adjust heat so fat does not burn, but the meat becomes crisp and golden. Lift out scallops, drain on paper towels, and transfer to a warmed serving platter; keep hot. Add more butter to the pan, as necessary, and sauté remaining scallops.

When all are cooked, wipe out the skillet and add remaining butter to the pan. Heat until butter begins to smell nutty and turns light brown. Squeeze remaining lemon half and stir in the juice. Remove pan from heat and trickle the lemon butter over the scallops. Garnish the center of each scallop with a lemon slice and a curled anchovy fillet topped with an olive. Sprinkle with capers if you use them. At either side of the dish arrange small piles of egg white, parsley and egg yolk. Serve immediately.

Variations: For veal Holstein top the sautéed scallops with a fried egg and garnish with anchovy fillets. For veal Zingara top the sautéed scallops with a mixture of ham, tongue and mushrooms, all cut into matchsticks, lightly tossed in melted butter and moistened with Madeira sauce. For veal Milanaise serve the sautéed scallops with cooked spaghetti tossed in butter with matchsticks of ham and tongue, flavored with grated cheese and moistened with tomato sauce.

Veal Scaloppini with Marsala

4 portions

1 **pound small veal scallops**	1 **tablespoon olive oil**
seasoned flour	¼ **cup chicken stock**
5 **tablespoons unsalted**	½ **cup Marsala wine**
butter	

Prepare and flatten the scallops. Coat them lightly with seasoned flour, shaking off any excess. Heat 2 tablespoons of the butter and the oil in a large heavy pan. Put in several scallops, but do not crowd the pan. Sauté over brisk heat for about 2 minutes on each side, until scallops are golden. Adjust heat to keep the veal sizzling but do not let the butter burn. Lift out veal, drain over the pan, arrange on a serving dish, and keep hot while sautéing the rest of the scallops in batches. Add a little more butter (reserving 2 tablespoons) to the pan between batches, as necessary.

When all the scallops are cooked, pour the stock and Marsala into the pan and boil over high heat for at least 1 minute, scraping up the juices from the pan. Remove pan from heat and stir in remaining butter, little by little, to enrich the sauce and thicken it lightly. Check the seasoning and pour the sauce over the scallops. Serve immediately.

Sautéed Veal with Wine and Olive Oil

4 portions

1¼ pounds fillet of veal
2 garlic cloves
¼ cup olive oil
3 bay leaves

salt and black pepper
5 tablespoons dry white wine
   or dry vermouth

If the butcher has not done this already, cut the veal into very thin slices and flatten them as for scallops. When you are ready to cook, pat veal slices dry and cut them into 1-inch pieces. Divide the meat into 2 or 3 batches to avoid crowding the pan. Peel garlic cloves. Pour 3 tablespoons of the oil into a heavy frying pan. Add peeled garlic cloves and bay leaves. Warm over low heat to flavor the oil. Remove pan from heat, add 1 batch of meat, and stir well to coat the meat with oil. Increase heat, replace pan over heat and sauté veal briskly for 3 to 4 minutes, stirring frequently until veal turns pale and is

just cooked through. Remove from heat and lift out the meat, allowing excess fat to run back into the pan. Transfer the meat to a hot serving dish and season with salt and pepper. Cook the rest of the veal in the same manner, adding more oil to the pan only if necessary.

After cooking the last batch of meat, discard the garlic and bay leaves. Add the wine to the pan and heat briskly, scraping the pan, until liquid is reduced to a syrupy consistency. Spoon the sauce over the meat and serve at once.

Pork Tenderloin with Prunes

6 portions

18	large prunes	4	tablespoons unsalted butter
2	cups dry white wine	2	tablespoons oil
3	pork tenderloins, each 12 ounces	2	tablespoons red-currant jelly
¾	cup seasoned flour	¾	cup heavy cream

Soak the prunes overnight in 1 cup of the wine. Next day, pour prunes and wine into a saucepan and simmer gently for 10 to 15 minutes, until prunes are tender and plump. Remove prunes from heat but keep them warm.

Trim any skin or fat from the pork and wipe with a damp cloth. With a sharp knife cut the fillets across into diagonal slices about 1 inch thick. Lay the pieces on a board and flatten them slightly by beating with a cleaver or rolling pin. Spread the seasoned flour on a sheet of wax paper and turn the pieces of pork in it until lightly coated, shaking off excess flour.

Heat 2 tablespoons of the butter and 1 tablespoon of the oil in a wide sauté pan over moderate heat. When the fat is hot, put in the pork slices, in a single uncrowded layer. Sauté pork over high heat for 2 to 3 minutes, until lightly browned. Turn the slices and brown the other side. Reserve browned slices in a warm place. Sauté the rest of the pork in batches, adding more butter and oil to the pan as necessary. When all the pieces of pork are browned, return them to the pan. Add remaining wine, bring to a boil, and boil for 1 minute. Lower the heat, cover the pan lightly, and simmer for about 20 minutes, until the meat is very tender. Lift out the meat with a slotted spoon, let it drain over the pan for a second, then arrange in the center of an oval serving dish. Keep hot.

Drain the wine from the prunes into the sauté pan and boil, uncovered, stirring and scraping the juices from the bottom of the pan, until liquid is reduced to about ½ cup. Add the red-currant jelly and stir until dissolved. Add the cream, stir, and continue heating gently, shaking the pan now and then, until the sauce is thickened enough to coat a spoon. Check the seasoning and pour the sauce over the meat. Arrange the warm prunes on either side of the dish. Serve immediately.

Southern Fried Chicken

6 portions

1	frying chicken, 3½ pounds salt and white pepper	1	teaspoon paprika
3	cups milk	1	to 2 cups lard or vegetable shortening
1½	cups flour		

Cut chicken into 6 portions, leaving part of the breast on each wing. (Save back and neck for stock.) Put the pieces in a glass or ceramic bowl, sprinkle with salt and white pepper, and pour in 1 cup of the milk. Turn chicken so all pieces are moistened. Cover and refrigerate overnight.

At cooking time remove chicken from the milk and drain it. Pour 1 cup of the flour and the paprika into a brown paper bag and shake the chicken, one piece at a time, in the flour until well coated. Use more of the flour if needed. Melt the lard or shortening in a large heavy skillet; use enough of the fat to make a layer about ¾ inch deep. Increase the heat and add all the chicken. After 3 minutes reduce heat to moderate and cover the skillet. Panfry chicken for 10 minutes, then uncover and turn the pieces over with tongs. Panfry for 10 minutes longer, or until the pieces are all golden brown and crisp on the outside, and tender inside.

Remove white meat pieces as soon as they are tender; legs may need a few minutes longer. Pile the cooked chicken on a platter covered with several layers of paper towels and keep warm while making gravy.

Pour off all but 3 tablespoons of the fat in the pan. Spoon in 2 tablespoons flour and let it brown, stirring. Pour in remaining 2 cups milk. Over low heat scrape the skillet to release all the browned juices and continue to mix until the gravy is thick. Season to taste. Transfer chicken to a warmed dry platter and serve the gravy in a bowl.

Note: This is most like a Virginia dish; in Georgia chicken is not soaked at all; in Florida it is soaked in salt water and cooked in bacon fat and butter. Each region has its own version of this typical panfried dish.

Pork Chops with Wine

4 portions

4	pork chops
	salt and black pepper
½	cup flour
2	teaspoons oil
½	cup dry white or rosé wine

1	tablespoon prepared Dijon-style mustard
4	teaspoons capers
¼	cup chicken stock

Trim skin and excess fat from the chops. Wipe chops with a damp cloth. Sprinkle both sides lightly with salt and pepper and dust with the flour.

Heat a large heavy skillet over moderate heat and brush it with oil. When very hot, put in the chops and cook over fairly high heat until lightly browned on one side, 2 to 3 minutes. Turn the chops and brown the other side. Pour off any fat that has run from the chops (there may not be any if the chops are lean). Add the wine and let it boil briskly for a minute or two. Lower the heat, cover the pan tightly, and cook the chops gently for 10 to 15 minutes, until meat is tender. Lift out chops, arrange them on a serving dish, and keep warm.

Raise the heat to moderate and stir the mustard, capers and stock into the pan juices. Simmer for several minutes until well reduced. Check the seasoning. Pour the sauce over the chops and serve immediately.

Stir-Fried Pork and Spinach

2 portions

8	ounces pork tenderloin
1	pound fresh spinach, or 1 package (10 ounces) frozen spinach
3	tablespoons vegetable oil
2	tablespoons soy sauce

1	tablespoon dry sherry wine
1	teaspoon sugar
½	teaspoon black pepper
3	tablespoons vegetable shortening
1	teaspoon salt

Cut the pork tenderloin into julienne strips. Wash spinach, trim, drain well, and chop. Heat the oil in a large saucepan over moderate heat. When hot, add pork strips and stir-fry for 2 minutes. Add the soy sauce, sherry, sugar and black pepper and continue to stir-fry for 2 minutes longer. With a slotted spoon transfer the pork to a plate.

Add 2 tablespoons of the vegetable shortening to the pan and melt over moderate heat. Add the spinach and salt to the pan and stir-fry the mixture for 3 minutes. Add remaining shortening to the pan and continue to stir-fry for 30 seconds. With a slotted spoon, transfer spinach to a warmed serving dish. Increase the heat and return pork strips to the pan. Stir-fry for 30 seconds, to reheat them completely. Pour pork and pan juices over the spinach and serve at once.

Stir-Fried Chicken with Wine-Cream Sauce

4 portions

4	boned chicken breasts, skinned
¼	teaspoon ground ginger
1½	teaspoons salt
1	teaspoon black pepper
1	tablespoon cornstarch
1	small red bell pepper
½	cucumber
1	tablespoon butter
2	tablespoons vegetable oil
4	ounces shelled small shrimps

Wine-Cream Sauce

6	tablespoons chicken stock
1	tablespoon butter
¼	cup dry white wine
1	tablespoon cornstarch
¼	cup water
½	cup light cream

Prepare chicken for stir-frying (see Index), then cut the strips into cubes. Rub the pieces with the ginger, salt, pepper and cornstarch. Set aside. Wash red pepper, discard stem, seeds and ribs, and cut pepper into ½-inch strips. Peel cucumber, halve it, remove seeds, and cut into ½-inch pieces. Melt the butter with the oil in a wok or large skillet over moderate heat. Add the chicken cubes and stir-fry for 30 seconds. Add the shrimps, red pepper and cucumber to the pan and stir-fry the mixture for 2 minutes. Remove pan from heat and set aside.

Make the sauce: Bring the chicken stock to a boil in a small saucepan over moderate heat. Stir in the butter and wine and simmer until the butter is melted. Reduce heat to low. Stir cornstarch into ¼ cup cold water; add to the sauce, stirring constantly. Simmer sauce for 2 minutes, until thickened. Add the cream and stir until well blended. Pour the sauce into the wok or skillet. Return pan to moderate heat and cook the mixture, turning the meat and vegetables over in the sauce, for 2 minutes. Remove pan from heat and pour the mixture into a warmed serving dish. Serve at once.

Sweet-and-Sour Chicken

2 portions

8 ounces boned chicken breast
½ teaspoon salt
½ teaspoon cornstarch
3 tablespoons corn oil
1 ounce bamboo shoots
1 green pepper
1 small onion
1 ounce gingerroot
1 garlic clove

Sweet-and-Sour Sauce

1 tablespoon soy sauce
1 tablespoon red-wine vinegar
1 tablespoon brown sugar
1 tablespoon tomato purée
¼ cup chicken stock

Cut chicken breast into thin slices. Mix together the salt and cornstarch and rub the mixture into the sliced chicken. Heat the oil in a wok or large skillet over moderate heat. Spread the sliced chicken in a single layer in the wok. Stir-fry for 4 minutes to cook the chicken. Remove chicken from pan, drain on paper towels, and set aside in a warm place.

Slice the bamboo shoots. Wash pepper, discard stem, seeds and ribs, and cut pepper into thin slices. Peel and chop the onion. Peel and mince the gingerroot and garlic. Mix all the sauce ingredients together in a small bowl.

Return the wok or skillet to the heat. Add the bamboo shoots, green pepper, onion, garlic and gingerroot, and stir-fry over moderate heat for 1 minute. Return chicken to the pan, pour in the sauce, and mix chicken with the sauce so that each piece is coated. Cook for 1 minute, then serve.

Chicken San Marino

6 portions

6 boned chicken-breast halves, skinned
¼ cup seasoned flour
4 ounces butter
8 large mushrooms
8 slices of mozzarella cheese

Place the chicken pieces between 2 sheets of wax paper or plastic wrap on a work surface and pound them with a mallet, cleaver or rolling pin until thin. Put the seasoned flour on a large plate and dip the chicken-breast halves into the mixture until well coated. Melt 3 ounces of the butter in a large skillet over moderate heat. Add chicken pieces, a few at a time, and cook for 4 to 5 minutes on each side. Transfer chicken to a shallow flameproof casserole.

Preheat broiler to high. Wipe mushrooms with a damp cloth, trim base of stems, and slice caps and stems.

Melt remaining butter in the same skillet and add mushrooms. Sauté them for 1 to 2 minutes, until they have been just coated with the butter. Arrange mushroom slices on top of the chicken and cover each piece with a slice of mozzarella cheese. Place the casserole under the broiler for about 3 minutes, until the mozzarella has melted and is beginning to brown. Serve very hot.

Sautéed Chicken

4 portions

1 frying chicken, 3½ pounds
  salt and black pepper
4 tablespoons unsalted butter
1 tablespoon oil
3 shallots or 2 green onions (scallions)
¼ cup dry white vermouth
⅔ cup chicken stock
1 teaspoon soy sauce
4 teaspoons chopped fresh parsley

49

Cut the chicken into 8 pieces. Dry them thoroughly on paper towels. Sprinkle the skin lightly with salt and pepper.

Heat 2 tablespoons of the butter and the oil in a sauté pan over moderate heat. Put in the chicken pieces, skin side down, in a single layer. If necessary, sauté in 2 batches rather than crowd the pan. Sauté over slightly higher heat. When chicken has browned on one side, in 2 or 3 minutes, turn and brown another surface. Repeat every 2 minutes until all surfaces are golden. Keep the heat regulated so the chicken sizzles and browns but the fat does not burn. If the fat should burn, lift out the chicken pieces, discard all the fat, and heat fresh butter and oil before proceeding.

Peel and chop the shallots or green onions. When chicken is browned, add vegetables to the pan. Cover pan and reduce the heat to a gentle simmer. After 10 to 12 minutes, test the white meat pieces by piercing with a fine skewer. If the juices run clear, transfer those pieces to a serving dish and keep warm. Continue cooking the dark meat for 4 to 5 minutes longer. When cooked, add these to the white meat pieces. Skim off excess fat, leaving about 1 tablespoon in the pan, with the chopped shallot or green onion and any juices from the chicken pieces. Add vermouth and stock. Increase the heat and boil rapidly, uncovered, scraping up the browned juices, until liquid is reduced to about half.

Remove pan from heat; add the soy sauce and parsley. Cut remaining 2 tablespoons of butter into small pieces and beat into the sauce, bit by bit, to enrich and thicken it. Check the seasoning, spoon the sauce over the chicken, and serve at once.

Variations: For chicken with tarragon, add a large sprig of fresh tarragon when deglazing the pan. After reducing the stock and vermouth, remove tarragon sprig and add ¼ cup heavy cream and 1 tablespoon minced fresh tarragon. Simmer for a minute or two, check seasoning, and pour over the chicken.

For chicken Georgina, substitute 12 peeled small white onions and a small *bouquet garni* for the shallots or scallions. When chicken is browned and cooked, discard the *bouquet garni* and deglaze the pan with 4 tablespoons mushroom cooking liquid and 4 tablespoons dry white vermouth. Boil rapidly until reduced by half. Add 12 trimmed button mushrooms and ½ cup heavy cream. Simmer gently until the sauce begins to thicken. Check the seasoning and pour sauce over the chicken pieces.

Fried Marinated White Fish

4 portions

1 pound white fish (shark, haddock, cod)	10 anchovy fillets
juice of 1 lemon	3 tablespoons olive oil
1 teaspoon dry mustard	1 tablespoon chopped fresh parsley
½ teaspoon freshly ground black pepper	3 tablespoons flour
½ teaspoon dried orégano	6 tablespoons oil, for frying
	1 large egg

Remove any bones from the fish and cut it into 2-inch lengths. In a large glass or ceramic bowl mix together the lemon juice, mustard, black pepper and orégano. Mince the anchovy fillets and add to the marinade with the olive oil and parsley. Mix well. Add the fish and stir gently for a few seconds to cover all the pieces of fish with the marinade. Cover the dish loosely and leave in a cool place for 1 to 2 hours.

Remove the fish from the marinade with a slotted spoon, allowing excess liquid to drain back into the bowl. Reserve the marinade. Spread the flour on a sheet of wax paper. Roll each piece of fish in flour to coat thoroughly and shake to remove any excess.

Pour the frying oil into a skillet and heat until a cube of bread dropped into the oil turns golden in about 30 seconds. Beat the egg lightly in a shallow bowl. Dip the fish, piece by piece, into the beaten egg to coat lightly, and immediately lower the fish into the hot oil. Do not crowd the pan. Fry for 2 to 3 minutes, turning once or twice, until pieces are golden and crisp. Lift out the fish with a slotted spoon, drain briefly on paper towels, and arrange the pieces on a hot serving dish. Keep hot and continue with remaining fish.

Just before serving, sprinkle the fried fish with a little of the marinade.

Trout with Almonds

4 portions

4 fresh trout, each 8 ounces	2 ounces slivered blanched almonds
¼ cup seasoned flour	1 tablespoon lemon juice
6 tablespoons clarified butter	salt and black pepper
2 tablespoons raw butter	

Coat the fish with the seasoned flour, shaking off any excess flour. Heat 3 tablespoons clarified butter in a large skillet; when butter is hot, put in 2 trout and panfry gently over moderate heat for 4 to 5 minutes, until golden. Turn the fish carefully and cook on the other side for 4 to 5 minutes. Check that the fish is cooked through to the bone by making a small incision with the point of a knife in the thickest part. Lift the fish out without draining, arrange on a serving dish, and keep hot. Add remaining clarified butter to the pan and cook the next 2 fish in the same manner.

When all the fish are cooked, remove pan from heat and wipe out with paper towels. Put in the raw butter and return pan to the heat. When butter is hot, sauté the almonds, stirring frequently, until golden brown. Add the lemon juice to the pan with a light seasoning of salt and pepper. Stir, spoon over the trout, and serve immediately.

Cod Provençal Style

4 portions

1½ pounds cod fillets	¼ cup olive oil
2 tablespoons seasoned flour	1 teaspoon chopped fresh parsley
1 medium-size onion	salt and black pepper
2 garlic cloves	¼ cup pitted black olives
1 pound tomatoes	

Skin the fillets and cut into 1½-inch squares. Spoon the seasoned flour into a plastic bag. Add the fish, a piece at a time, and toss until well coated. Remove fish and shake off excess flour. Peel and slice the onion; peel and crush the garlic cloves; peel, seed, and chop the tomatoes.

Heat 2 tablespoons oil in a sauté pan over low heat. When hot, put in the onion and cook gently for 6 to 8 minutes, until soft. Add the garlic and cook for another minute or two; then add the tomatoes, chopped parsley, and salt and pepper to taste. Toss over fairly high heat for several minutes, until the tomatoes begin to soften; then reduce heat to minimum and cover the pan.

Heat remaining oil in a large skillet. When sizzling hot, put in the pieces of fish. Panfry over moderate heat, turning frequently, until cooked through and lightly browned on both sides, about 8 minutes. Remove fish with a slotted spoon, drain on paper towels, and transfer to a warmed serving dish. Spoon the vegetables over the fish, garnish with black olives, and serve immediately.

Part Three

VEGETABLES: BASIC COOKING METHODS

"Never would it occur to a child that sheep, pigs, cows or chickens were good to eat, while, like Milton's *Adam,* he would readily make a meal off fruit, nuts, thyme, mint, peas and broad beans, which penetrate further and stimulate not only the appetite but other vague and deep nostalgias. We are closer to the Vegetable Kingdom than we know; is it not for us alone that mint, thyme, sage, and rosemary exhale 'crush me and eat me!' . . . Their aim is to be absorbed by man, although they can achieve it only by attaching themselves to roast mutton."

Cyril Connolly
The Unquiet Grave

Oddly enough, today we have come to accept as commonplace the notion that children hate vegetables. Day in, day out, frustrated parents everywhere confront, command, cajole, implore, threaten and beg their children to "eat your vegetables. . . . Eat them because they're good for you! Eat them because they make you strong! Eat them because they make you healthy!" All this, and usually to no avail. Not much can budge a stubborn child who has set his mind against a dish of food. M. F. K. Fisher eloquently describes the situation: "When a man is small, he loves and hates food with a ferocity which soon dims. At six years old his very bowels will heave when such a dish as creamed carrots or cold tapioca appears before him. His throat will close, and spots of nausea and rage swim in his vision. It is hard, later, to remember why, but at the time there is no pose in his disgust" *(Serve it Forth).*

The fact is that children genuinely do like vegetables, although it's true that they are particular about the way their vegetables are prepared.

They will happily eat carrots any number of ways: traditional and most popular is a whole carrot, washed and scraped but otherwise unchanged; or carrots can be cut into julienne sticks, sliced into rounds and even shredded, and if they must be cooked then do it only minimally so they retain their crunchy texture and brilliant orange color.

The same applies to celery. Children enjoy its naturally salty taste and crisp refreshing texture. They'll munch away at stalks or neatly cut-up matchsticks, and may even try a nibble of the slightly bitter leaf. But cook celery till it is mushy and muck it up with sticky sauce, and it will invariably be pushed aside.

Even zucchini appeals to children despite its slightly foreign name. It too is good when just barely steamed so that the sweet mild flesh retains a little crunch.

Sweet, succulent bell peppers—red, yellow, green—make colorful appealing snacks as does the licorice-flavored fennel bulb.

Wholesome broccoli, cauliflower and cabbage are all more pleasing to the taste and tooth when served just slightly undercooked.

The point is that children dislike vegetables that have been overdone, or too much fussed with, or disguised. Their unspoiled taste buds and healthy natural instincts lead them to reject soggy, overcooked vegetables, which are so often served to them—vegetables with little taste and even fewer nutrients.

Many of the routine tasks involving the preparation of fresh vegetables provide excellent opportunities for involving small children in the kitchen and thereby helping them to expand the range of foods that they will try as well as their knowledge of cooking procedures, and even facts about history and geography.

Julia Child, a great proponent of early childhood participation in the kitchen, writes that "The small rituals, like clean hands and clean apron before setting to work; the precision of gesture, like leveling off a cupful of flour; the charm of improvisation and making something new; the pride of mastery; and the gratification of offering something one has made—these have such value to a child. And where are they so easily to be obtained as in cooking? The patience and good humor demanded of you by cooking with a child are a good investment" *(Julia Child & Company)*.

There is great charm in mundane tasks like shelling peas if we can learn to take the time to enjoy the quality of discovery and wonder that is the birthright of the child. Always remember that an activity we consider routine can be a memorable experience for children. So let us not neglect simple pleasures like those involved in shelling peas. Show children how to snap off an end, pull down the string along the side, just like a zipper on a seam, and pop the peas into a bowl. Some children are amazed when they discover that this is nature's way of packaging the pea; that peas don't always come frozen together in a box or bag.

This cozy kitchen situation is perfect for encouraging the practice of tasting things as you work along. It is the habits of tasting, noticing, observing and comparing that in the long run are what make someone a natural cook and not just a follower of recipes. You might notice that the peas that you are shelling are not all uniform in size; some are tiny, almost unformed, and others are large and plumply round. But do they taste the same? Aren't the small ones just a little sweeter? Aren't some of the really big ones lacking in flavor? If the peas are very fresh, sweet, juicy, tender, then you might well consider just how long they should be cooked. All this can be discussed, testing and tasting as you go. Perhaps you will discover for yourselves that just a few minutes of light steaming and then a tiny bit of butter and a snip or two of mint is all you need to turn peas into a tasty feast. This kind of practical, firsthand experience will benefit the lucky child with a lifetime of good eating, and perhaps he will have for himself discovered that peas need not be "yucky" after all.

Buy the smallest, freshest snap beans, so fresh and crisp that when you bend them they break with a most satisfying snap. Enlist a child to help you top them, tail them, and taste them also as you work along. Steam them or boil them quickly, briefly, and watch together as their color turns to an amazing, brilliant emerald green. Toss them in olive oil and lemon juice while they are warm and eat them with some crusty bread. That is how vegetables were meant to be eaten.

Take a child shopping to a greengrocer or farmer's market where vegetables are sold unwrapped in cellophane, plastic or styrofoam. Together choose the smallest new potatoes, the littlest zucchini, fresh beets no larger than a marble, green snap beans as thin as matchsticks....At home, prepare them quickly, cook them briefly, and eat them together to discover one of the most important truths of all: when buying vegetables or fruits, biggest is not necessarily the best.

Everyone knows that vegetables are good for you. Indeed, for hundreds of years many vegetables were considered more of a medicine than a food, and were prescribed by herbalists to remedy various illnesses and to prevent others. According to Jane Grigson, it was not until the late 1700s that "...certain plants, their leaves, fruits and roots, had escaped from the black bag of antique medicine" *(Jane Grigson's Vegetable Book).* But vegetables can only nourish the body if they are eaten. To that end they must be prepared in such a way that they delight the eye and please the palate.

VEGE-TABLES: BASIC COOKING METHODS

Vegetables taste best if they are washed, prepared, cooked and served in quick succession. The whole process does not take long, so do everything as near as possible to mealtime. Try to avoid preparing vegetables in advance, or cooking ahead and reheating them.

Most vitamins and minerals are heat-soluble, or water-soluble, or both. This means some goodness is inevitably lost as soon as vegetables go into the cooking pot (which is one of the reasons why nutritionists are always urging us to eat more uncooked vegetables), but loss can be minimized by brief and careful cooking. Two of the quickest and best methods are boiling and steaming. Follow the basic rules given here and you will enjoy vegetables that look and taste delicious and are genuinely good for you!

Boiling

Boiling is an excellent way to cook vegetables. It is so quick that few nutrients are lost, and this means maximum flavor and color are also retained. But to call this cooking process boiling is slightly misleading because, for best results, vegetables should in fact be cooked at a gentle simmer.

To cover or not to cover: Do not cover green vegetables, for the moisture that rises to the lid condenses and drops down, changing the color from its natural green to an unpleasant color. Also, in the case of acid vegetables such as spinach, the flavor is altered as well. Other vegetables may be cooked covered or not, but you must watch closely for in the closed pot it is easy to overcook them. To cook covered, a pan with a well-fitting lid is essential. Not only does it save fuel and prevent cooking smells escaping, it also prevents valuable vitamins, which rise in the form of steam, from evaporating into the atmosphere.

In all cases stainless-steel, nonstick finish, hard enamel or aluminum pans are preferable. Copper pans should not be used; they destroy vitamin C on contact. Poor-quality, soft enamel pans should also be avoided. They are inclined to chip and wear at the seams, which can release harmful salts of antimony into food. The size of pan depends on the amount of vegetables you plan to cook. Choose the smallest pan possible; this means there will be less water to dissolve valuable vitamins.

There's no need to use lots of water; in fact it is preferable to use only enough to cover the vegetables. Add salt, just a pinch; too much will encourage vegetable juices to leak out. Never add baking soda; it may help to preserve green colors but it destroys vitamins, especially thiamine, and makes vegetables mushy.

The water should be at the boiling point when you add vegetables because the water at this temperature retains the vitamin C as much as possible and also slightly intensifies green colors.

Keep heat high and bring the water back to a boil as quickly as possible after adding the vegetable. Then reduce the heat and simmer the vegetable gently.

Simmering will cook vegetables just as fast as boiling; it saves fuel; also, because it causes less bumping around in the pan, vegetables keep their shapes better.

Vegetables are cooked as soon as they are tender; it takes less time to reach this stage than many people imagine. It is a good idea to stand by the stove while vegetables cook so you can catch them at the exact minute

Boiling Vegetables

1 Salt the water and bring it to a full rolling boil.

4 If cooking in a covered pan, lower the heat so that the water is just simmering.

7 If cooking a leafy vegetable, such as cabbage, extract excess water with a vegetable press.

they are done to your taste. Test with a skewer or fork, or lift a piece from the pan to taste. Never leave vegetables to cook until soft: they will lose flavor and vitamins and, if they are cooked in boiling water, they are liable to become soggy and waterlogged.

Drain boiled vegetables thoroughly as soon as cooked; save the liquid for gravies, health drinks or

2 Add the prepared vegetables.

3 Cover the pan until the water returns to a boil. Remove lid if recipe states to boil uncovered.

5 Near the end of cooking time, test the vegetables with a skewer or kitchen fork.

6 Remove from heat and drain the vegetables in a colander.

8 Return vegetables to the cleaned pan and put briefly over low heat to evaporate excess moisture.

9 Stir in butter, pepper and other flavorings. Turn into a warm dish and serve immediately.

to taste, turn into a warm vegetable dish, and serve as soon as possible.

Vitamins and minerals will be lost from vegetables if they are kept hot for any length of time. Green vegetables, especially cabbage family species, will start to smell unpleasant as well.

If you do have to keep cooked vegetables waiting, the best way to do it is to drain the vegetables as soon as they are cooked, refresh them by pouring cold water over them, and drain again. Cover them and set aside until needed. To reheat, put the vegetables into a shallow pan without any water and heat gently until the steam stops rising; or toss them in a little butter or oil.

This last cooking procedure, called blanching and refreshing (*rafraîchir* in French), is undoubtedly the best method for all green vegetables, even if you plan to serve them at once. Drain them from the boiling (blanching) water when they are tender but still somewhat crisp and still bright green. (If the color has altered, you have already cooked the vegetable too long.) Pour the drained vegetable into a bowl of very cold water, even ice water, or rinse with cold water, and drain again. The cold rinse stops all enzyme action and sets the color, so it remains bright even during reheating. Also the quick chilling ends all cooking action and helps keep the texture. This works for all leafy greens and for asparagus, broccoli, Brussels sprouts, green beans, peas. Because of the effect on enzyme action, it is a useful method for most vegetables, even if they are not green.

stocks. Many cooks claim they can drain vegetables by lifting the lid a little, tilting the pan, and letting the liquid pour out, but this is far from satisfactory. For quicker and more effective results always tip the vegetables into a colander or a sieve (metal colanders are strongest and last longer than plastic ones); drain off liquid. Leafy vegetables, such as spinach and shredded cabbage, which absorb water easily, benefit from being lightly squeezed with a vegetable press or the back of a wooden spoon to release surplus liquid.

Return drained vegetables to the cleaned-out pan and place over very low heat for a few seconds to evaporate any remaining excess moisture. Then add butter, season with salt and pepper

Steaming

Steaming is an excellent alternative method to ensure that vegetables are properly cooked and retain shape and texture; because they are not immersed in water, they never become waterlogged.

There are two ways of steaming: open steaming and closed steaming. Open steaming means that the vegetables are placed in a perforated con-

Steaming Vegetables

tainer over a pan of bubbling hot water so that they are cooked by the steam penetrating the holes in the container. Closed steaming means that the vegetables are placed in a solid container, or wrapped in foil, over a pan of bubbling water, and the steam does not touch the vegetables at all. The container is heated by the rising steam from the pan and the heat cooks the vegetables.

The open method cooks vegetables more quickly than the closed, but the closed method preserves even more of the original flavor. Any juices that seep out of the vegetables during cooking are trapped in the container rather than escaping into the cooking water.

The amount of water placed in the pan depends on which steaming method you are using. With the open method, very little water is needed; it must never bubble up through the holes and touch the vegetables. With the closed method, the water should come about halfway up the vegetable container.

Always wait until the water is boiling and the steam rising before you put the vegetables in the steamer. Once vegetables are in the steamer, cover immediately or steam will escape into the air and vegetables will take too long to cook. A fast boil is not necessary; save fuel by keeping the water bubbling gently; just as much steam will rise.

A double boiler can be used for the closed method of steaming. However, sealing the vegetables in foil in an open steamer will produce the same result. The foil is exposed directly to the steam so that the vegetables will cook faster than in the double boiler.

Another "steaming" method is one-pot steaming. This requires a heavy pan with a tight-fitting lid. Vegetables are placed in the pan with just enough water to cover the bottom of the pan; sometimes a pat of butter is added. The pan is covered, the heat is lowered and the vegetables, which have been lightly salted, start to give up their juices. This method is best used with vegetables with a high water con-

1 Put water in the pan and position steamer basket. Water must not come through the holes.

OR If using a closed steamer, check there is enough water to come halfway up the sides of the inner pan.

4 Check the water level from time to time. Add boiling water if necessary.

5 If cooking a large amount of vegetables, turn them occasionally to ensure even cooking.

tent, such as zucchini or summer squash. This method is also suitable when a vegetable is cut into very small pieces, such as shredded carrots.

Steamers

Flower steamer. This is the cheapest type of steamer to buy and is first-rate providing you use a saucepan with a well-fitting lid. The sides are perforated petals hinged to a perforated base, which stands on 3 or 4 legs to raise it clear of the water so that only the steam penetrates the holes and cooks the vegetables. You can open the petals wide like a full-blown flower or close them tight like a bud, depending on how many vegetables and what

size pan you are using. These are available in aluminum and stainless steel.

Chinese steamers. These are basketwork containers with solid sides, open-weave bases and their own lids. They are designed to fit on top of a small saucepan. You can build a "tower block" of several containers with a lid on the top one, which is ideal for steaming small portions of several different vegetables. Chinese steamers can be bought from most Chinese supermarkets, kitchen supply stores and mail-order houses.

Double boiler. This is a set of two saucepans, one fitting on top or just inside the other, with one lid. You pour water into the larger, bottom saucepan, and put vegetables in the

2 Bring water to a boil. Put vegetables in the steamer, cover, and return to the boil.

3 Lower heat immediately so the water simmers gently but steam is still rising.

6 Test the vegetables with a skewer or fork to see if they are tender in the center.

7 Turn the vegetables into a serving dish. Add butter and season to taste.

Oven temperature and position can vary for baking vegetables, although 350° to 400°F is the usual range. To test for doneness, insert a skewer or thin knife into the center; the pulp should feel soft.

Roasting

Everyone loves potatoes roasted around the meat; for many cooks, that is where vegetable roasting ends. Many root vegetables can also be roasted: carrots, onions, leeks, turnips, parsnips. Roast vegetables are an excellent accompaniment to meat and fish dishes. The addition of cheese, sliced ham or bacon to roasted vegetables will make a meal.

Apart from roasting vegetables with meat or poultry, they can be cooked along with a casserole to utilize the oven heat. Rather than roasting just one vegetable, combine several kinds for taste and variety.

If vegetables are to be roasted along with meat or poultry, wait until there is sufficient fat accumulated before adding them to the pan. Parboiling the vegetables is necessary if the roast will be finished before the vegetables would be crisp on the outside and soft inside. If the vegetables are being roasted by themselves, fat will have to be added to the pan. The fat can be butter or margarine, rendered chicken, beef or goose fat, bacon or flavored pork fat. Heat the fat before adding vegetables to the pan; the fat should be sizzling. Roast most vegetables in the center of the oven at 350°F. Roast potatoes at 425°F for maximum flavor and crispness. Be sure to baste the vegetables from time to time, turning them so that all sides are exposed to the oven heat.

Combine different vegetables, adding those that need the shortest cooking time last. Cut vegetables into slices or cubes, using different shapes for different vegetables to make a more interesting presentation. To glaze vegetables, such as carrots, onions or sweet-potato slices, sprinkle with brown sugar. Use salt, pepper and fresh herbs for added flavor.

upper pan, so the vegetables are cooked by the closed method of steaming.

Baking

Baking vegetables is a no-fuss way of cooking them; they need a minimum of preparation and the maximum flavor is preserved. Another plus is that the method yields vegetables less rich and lower in calories than if prepared by roasting with meat or poultry.

Select vegetables large enough to ensure a good proportion of flesh to skin, and of good quality so there are no hidden tough cores or bruised spots. Choose even-size vegetables so they will bake in the same time.

Pierce once or twice with a knife or fork before baking to prevent skins bursting. Bake without further preparation; or rub a little oil or butter over the skins to produce a juicy crispness rather than a dry finish. Do not use too much fat or the vegetables will roast rather than bake. If the skins are to be eaten, season with salt and pepper and flavor with herbs and spices.

Place the vegetables on a baking sheet or in a shallow casserole. A potato spike, with 6 or 8 prongs, speeds up the baking process since oven heat is conducted along the spike into the vegetable. Oil the prongs before pushing them into the vegetables. If your kitchen is not equipped with a potato spike, skewers will do.

Before serving, drain the vegetables, if necessary, on paper towels. However, try to keep the fat to a minimum so that the vegetables are barely coated.

Broiling

Broiling, sometimes called grilling, is the process of cooking vegetables under the broiler. Suitable vegetables are those that cook quickly, such as tomatoes, mushrooms, eggplant slices, strips of red or green peppers.

Brush the vegetables with clarified butter, or olive oil or cooking oil. Mushrooms are best brushed with butter. Tomatoes and peppers can be brushed with butter or oil. Eggplants should be brushed with oil. Salt, pepper and minced fresh herbs are a flavorful necessity.

Bread crumbs moistened with oil or melted butter make a nice topping. Grated Parmesan cheese or shredded mozzarella or other good melting cheeses make a flavorful addition.

VEGE-TABLES FOR COOKING

Steaming Vegetables

 Bamboo basket: Put washed, trimmed vegetables directly into steamer basket. Put water in wok and place basket inside wok.

2 Cover basket. Bring water in wok to a boil and steam vegetables according to recipe.

1 *Skillet steaming:* Place washed and trimmed asparagus in large-size skillet. Add ½ cup water.

 Cover skillet; place over high heat. Let water come to a boil and steam for 4 minutes.

Artichokes

Pick tightly closed green ones; heavy ones are moister. Allow one per person. Snap off stems and trim bottom; remove the outer leaves and cut off the top third. Rub all cut surfaces with a lemon half to prevent discoloration.

Boiling and Steaming. Place upright in a large pot. Add boiling water to cover, lemon slices and 1 teaspoon salt. Cook for 25 to 40 minutes, depending on size, until you can remove a leaf easily. Drain upside down and serve with melted butter. Artichokes can also be steamed for about the same amount of time.

Jerusalem Artichokes

Often called sunchokes. Allow 1 pound for 4 portions. Scrub them well; place in a bowl of cold water until ready to cook.

Boiling. Place in a pan of boiling salted water, cover, and boil for 8 to 10 minutes. Check near the end of the cooking. They must not be allowed to become soft, but just tender. Drain, peel, slice, and serve with butter.

Baking. Sunchokes can also be baked in a 400°F oven. You will need large ones, about 2 inches long and 1½ inches wide. Place them in a shallow baking pan in a preheated oven. Bake for 15 to 20 minutes, until just tender. Serve with butter, salt and pepper.

Asparagus

Look for tightly closed tips. Stalks with open or withered tips should not be

3 Remove wok from heat; take off basket lid. Season vegetables. Serve directly from basket or transfer to heated dish.

3 Remove pan lid; drain any excess liquid. Return skillet to low heat. Add butter and lemon juice. Transfer to heated serving platter.

bought. Store stalks upright in a container with water in the bottom and cover the heads with a plastic bag. Refrigerate until ready to cook. Allow 2 pounds for 4 to 6 portions.

Wash asparagus thoroughly to remove sand. Snap off bottoms and peel the skin from just below the tips to the end. Thick stalks should always be peeled. Thin ones often don't need peeling.

Boiling. Place asparagus flat in a large skillet, or any suitable flat pan, barely covered with salted, cold water. Bring to a boil, uncovered, and boil for 6 to 8 minutes, depending on size. Test by holding a stalk upright. The head should nod only slightly. They should be firm enough to eat with the fingers.

Steaming. Tie prepared stalks so they can stand upright. Use a special asparagus steamer, or place in the bottom pan of a double boiler with the top pan inverted over the bottom. Pour in about 1 inch of boiling salted water; cover and steam for a slightly longer time than for boiling. Test for doneness.

Serve drained asparagus with melted butter and lemon wedges, or with hollandaise sauce. Serve cold with vinaigrette sauce or mayonnaise.

Beans

Green beans used to be called string beans but since the strings have been bred out of them they are often called snap beans. Buy the smallest ones you can find. They should be crisp and easy to snap. Allow 2 pounds for 4 to 6 portions.

Wax beans, yellow in color, are prepared like green beans. Steaming is not suitable for beans.

Boiling. Pour plenty of salted water into a large saucepan and bring to a full boil. Add the beans gradually so the water continues to boil and cook, uncovered, for 10 to 15 minutes, depending on size. Taste for doneness. Beans should be crisp but not raw tasting.

Drain and serve with melted butter, salt and pepper. A few drops of lemon juice will enhance their flavor. Savory is a favorite herb for beans.

Variations: Toss with toasted, sliced almonds or thin-sliced water chestnuts. Serve cold with vinaigrette sauce or mustard-flavored mayonnaise.

Baby Lima Beans

Allow 3 pounds for 4 portions. Shell the limas, place in a large saucepan, and add boiling water and salt. Cover and simmer for 10 to 20 minutes, according to size. They should be soft and tender but not mushy. Drain and serve with butter, salt and pepper.

Broad Beans or Fava Beans

Similar to lima beans but bigger, often an inch in diameter. Cook like lima beans. Cool slightly and slip off the

Jerusalem Artichokes

1 Scrub the vegetables and cook whole in their skins. When tender, remove skin and cut off the woody ends.

2 If peeled before cooking, drop each into acidulated water until required. Cut off woody ends and slice if you like.

Preparing Asparagus

1 Wash stalks carefully in a basin of room-temperature water.

2 Scrape off scales, trim off woody ends, and scrape or peel stems with a vegetable peeler or sharp knife.

3 Tie stalks in bundles, each holding 1 portion. Tie in 2 places so the bundle will hold together during boiling/steaming.

---

heavy skins. Serve with butter, salt and pepper.

Beets

Small young ones are much more tender than the large old ones, which can sometimes be woody. Try to buy beets of uniform size. Allow about 2 pounds for 4 servings.

Wash beets well, but do not pierce the skin. Cut off all but 1½ inches of the tops; do not trim roots.

Baking. By far the most flavorful way of cooking. Wrap each beet in foil, the stem protruding. Bake in a preheated 450°F oven for 1½ to 2 hours, depending on size. The skins will slip off easily after they are cooked.

Serve tiny beets whole; slice or dice larger ones. Toss with butter, salt and pepper.

Boiling. Place prepared beets in a saucepan of boiling salted water. Cover and cook for 35 to 45 minutes, depending on size. Drop into cold water and peel.

Steaming. Beets can also be steamed but, because of their long cooking time, you will have to add boiling water to the pot as the cooking proceeds. Steaming will take about 1 hour.

Broccoli

Look for dark green or purple-tinted heads. Any that are yellowed or flowering are too old. The stalks should be crisp and moist. Allow 2 pounds for 4 to 6 portions.

Discard the leaves and the base of the stem. Peel the stems from the bottom up to the flowerets. Wash in cold water. The stems can be cut off and cooked separately. Peel them and slice them diagonally, or cut into julienne and combine them with carrots or green onions. The head should be divided into flowerets of equal size.

Steaming. Place in a steamer over boiling, salted water, or cook like asparagus, upright, with just the stems in water. Cover and cook for 10 to 12 minutes, until just tender but still crisp. Drain well.

Broccoli is also delicious blanched and refreshed.

Serve with melted butter and toasted sliced or slivered almonds. Or serve with hollandaise sauce, to which you have added grated orange rind and a teaspoon of orange juice. Serve with chopped garlic softened in a little olive oil, and garnish with chopped parsley. Or serve plain with lemon wedges.

Brussels Sprouts

Delicious when not overcooked. Look for firm heads and green color. Avoid those with withered outer leaves or a yellowish cast. Buy 2 pints for 4 portions.

Trim the stem slightly; make an X with the point of a knife in the base of each stem. Pull off any outer leaves that are discolored or dry. Soak in cold salted water for about 15 minutes.

Boiling. Cook the sprouts in boiling salted water to cover for about 10 minutes, until crisply tender. Drain and season with salt and pepper; add butter. Or omit butter and flavor with lemon juice and a pinch of nutmeg.

Cooking 1 pint of sprouts tossed with an equal amount of cooked chestnuts which have been heated in butter, will also serve 4.

Cabbage

There are different varieties of cabbage available in our markets. White cabbage has a firm, solid head. Green cabbage is smaller and more tender. Savoy cabbage is more loosely formed and more delicate in flavor, with crinkled leaves and pointed head. There is also red cabbage, often used raw in salads but delicious cooked. Red cabbage must always be cooked with an acid such as vinegar or red wine and usually a green apple so it keeps its red color.

Buy firm heavy heads with crisp leaves. A head of 2½ to 3 pounds will make 6 to 8 portions. Strip off and discard the outer leaves. Split the head into halves and cut out the core. The core can be sliced and used in salads. Cut cabbage into thin wedges, or slice or shred it.

Steaming. Cabbage retains its flavor best when cooked in about ½ inch of salted boiling water. Cover the pot tightly, lower the heat, and cook for about 4 minutes for shredded cabbage and for 6 to 8 minutes for wedges. When cabbage is crisp but tender, drain well and toss with melted butter. Season with pepper and salt, if necessary.

Carrots

Although we all know about raw carrots, there are many delicious ways to serve them cooked. Look for firm, bright-colored carrots. Avoid any that are cracked or split or have wilted tops. Buy 1½ to 2 pounds carrots for 4 portions.

Scrape the carrots, trim the tops and the tips, and slice across, on the diagonal or lengthwise. Tiny carrots can be left whole. Lengthwise strips can be cut into julienne.

Boiling. Place in boiling salted water to cover and cook until barely tender. The time will vary, depending on the cut, from 6 to 20 minutes. Drain them well, toss with butter, salt and pepper, and garnish with chopped parsley.

Variations: To glaze carrots, add 2 tablespoons of brown sugar or honey to the buttered carrots and cook over low heat, shaking the pan until they are glazed all over.

Shred raw carrots on the coarse side of a grater or in a food processor with the shredding disc. Cook, covered, in a heavy pan with 2 tablespoons butter, 2 tablespoons orange juice and ¼ teaspoon grated fresh gingerroot. Cook for about 5 minutes; uncover and quickly reduce any remaining liquid.

Cauliflower

Look for firm snowy heads and crisp green leaves. Buy 1 medium head, about 3 pounds, for 4 portions.

Remove green leaves, cut off the stem, and wash the head in cold water. If leaving it whole, cut an X in the base of the remaining stem to help even the cooking. The head can also be divided into flowerets, the stems trimmed to 1-inch size. Some cookbooks suggest adding a slice of lemon or a few tablespoons of milk to the cooking water to help keep the cauliflower white.

Boiling. Cook in boiling salted water to cover. Individual flowerets will take 5 to 6 minutes; a whole head will take from 12 to 20 minutes, depending on its size. Cook a head stem down. Tilt the pan to remove the head, and let it drain thoroughly.

Dress with melted butter and season with salt and pepper. Sprinkle with grated Parmesan cheese.

Celeriac or Celery Root

Sometimes called knob celery, this root vegetable is gradually becoming more available in markets. Although usually served raw in julienne strips, dressed with a mustard mayonnaise, it is delicious as a cooked vegetable. Since it is a difficult vegetable to peel, it is easier to scrub it well and cook it whole. Peeling is then much easier. There is much variation in size, and larger ones can be pithy inside. Look for knobs 2 to 4 inches in diameter. Buy 2 pounds to make 4 portions.

Boiling. Place scrubbed whole celery roots in boiling salted water and cook until tender, 30 to 40 minutes

depending on size. Drain well. Peel and slice or cube. Serve with melted butter, salt and pepper. Sprinkle with toasted bread crumbs and minced parsley.

Alternatively, place the cooked slices in a buttered flameproof dish, dot with butter, and sprinkle with grated cheese. A combination of Gruyère and Parmesan is nice. Place under the broiler until the cheese has melted and browned.

Corn

Corn loses flavor quickly so the fresher the better. Husks should be bright green and tight-fitting. The kernels should be plump and unwrinkled. The corn silk should be pale, not dried out. Remove the husks and the corn silk just before cooking the ears, not earlier. Break off the tip and trim the stem end.

Boiling. Never salt the water in which the corn is cooked. If the corn is old, add a tablespoon or two of sugar to the water. Place the shucked ears in a flat pan or large skillet, and cover them with cold water. Over high heat, bring the water to a full boil. Remove the corn and serve with butter, salt and pepper.

Eggplant

Available most of the year, this vegetable can be prepared by broiling, baking, steaming and frying. Instead of the usual large, dark purple eggplants, look for the small thin light purple ones, 4 to 6 inches long, or the round white ones. Pick eggplants with firm, shiny, unwrinkled skin and bright green leaves. About 1½ pounds will make 4 portions.

Wash well and remove the green cap. Slice unpeeled eggplant into rounds ½ inch thick.

Broiling. Preheat the broiler. Brush eggplant slices with about 2 tablespoons olive oil and broil about 4 inches from the source of heat until lightly browned. Turn the slices over, brush with more oil, and broil for 5 minutes longer. Sprinkle with salt and pepper. Serve with chopped parsley or

Preparing Leeks

1 Cut off leek roots and remove the tough portions of the green tops. Peel off tough outer leaves.

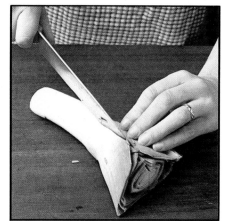

2 Split the leeks lengthwise to within 1 inch of the base.

3 Plunge into a basin of room-temperature water and gently open the layers to wash away all sand and grit.

---

top with grated Parmesan cheese or tomato sauce.

Baking. Prepare the eggplant and pierce the skin in 2 or 3 places with a skewer or knife tip. Bake in a preheated 350°F oven for about 1 hour. When cool enough to handle, peel eggplant and purée the pulp in a food processor or blender with 1 tablespoon lemon juice and 1 or 2 peeled garlic cloves. If you like things spicy, add a pinch of cayenne pepper. Reheat the purée with 1 to 2 tablespoons butter and garnish with chopped parsley; season with salt and pepper.

Eggplant slices can also be baked in foil in a 375°F oven. Wash and peel the eggplant. Cut into thick slices, ½ to ¾ inch; if the eggplant is very large, cut the slices into halves. Place each slice on a square of foil. Top with a slice of onion and a thick slice of tomato. Sprinkle with salt and pepper and a bit of minced fresh basil, if available. Fold the foil to seal the ingredients completely. Bake for about 20 minutes.

Steaming. Eggplant can be steamed in a steamer basket or colander over boiling water for 4 to 8 minutes.

Fennel

This native of the Mediterranean area is becoming easier to find in markets. It looks somewhat like fat short celery, has delicate feathery green tops, and tastes faintly of licorice. It is often sliced and eaten raw, but it is also delicious cooked. Look for crisp, plump bulbs with fresh feathery tops. Allow 1 bulb for each serving.

Peel the outer heavy ribs, cut off the tops, and cut crosswise into 1-inch slices, or cut lengthwise into quarters. Wash in cold water.

Boiling. Cook the fennel in boiling salted water in a covered pan until tender but still crisp, about 8 minutes for slices and 12 to 15 minutes for quartered bulbs. Drain well; toss with pepper and salt.

Greens

Beet greens, collards, chard, mustard greens, turnip greens, escarole and chicory are all nutritious and easy to prepare. Formerly these greens were cooked with salt pork, bacon, etc., for hours. These days, with the emphasis on crispness and retention of vitamins,

the cooking is completed in a far shorter time.

Wash all greens thoroughly in several changes of water; discard any faded or withered leaves.

Steaming. The water remaining on the leaves after washing is sufficient for cooking. Use a heavy saucepan with a tight-fitting lid. Over medium heat, let the greens cook until wilted. Beet greens will cook in 3 to 5 minutes. Collards will take 10 to 15 minutes. Chard, mustard greens, turnip greens, escarole and chicory will take 15 to 20 minutes. Very young leaves will take less time.

Drain the cooked greens; chop coarsely or leave whole. Serve with melted butter and lemon wedges. Or serve with crumbled crisp bacon and toss with a little bacon fat.

Leeks

The French call leeks the asparagus of the poor, but in this country they are definitely a luxury item with a rather high price. They have a delicate onion taste. Leeks come by the bunch, weighing about 2 pounds. Two bunches will make 4 portions. Occasionally they are sold singly; one large leek with greens may weigh 8 ounces. Leeks hold sandy dirt between the layers of leaves and must be washed thoroughly. When buying them, look for fresh green tops; the white portion should be crisp. Avoid those with yellowing or limp leaves.

Cut off the roots and the tough green tops, cutting to about 1 inch above the white bulb. Soak in water to loosen the dirt, then wash under running water, spreading the leaves to flush away the dirt. It may be necessary to split them almost all the way to the bottom to clean them.

Boiling. Cook leeks in a small amount of boiling salted water in a covered skillet until just tender, 12 to 15 minutes; if they are sliced or cut into julienne they will be tender in 5 to 8 minutes. Drain them well and serve with melted butter or hollandaise sauce. They are also delicious served cold with vinaigrette sauce.

Mushrooms

Although there are many species of mushrooms, most of us have access only to the cultivated white ones. Recently some fancier markets have been selling imported morels and chanterelles and the tiny shiitake. Imported dried mushrooms are also available in Oriental food stores and most supermarkets. These imported and dried mushrooms are quite expensive; save them for special dishes. When buying ordinary mushrooms, look for clean snowy ones. Avoid any that have had sodium bisulfite (a preservative) added, as these can look fresh and have a horrid taste. If you are serving raw mushrooms, either stuffed or sliced in a salad, you will want them white and snowy with closed caps covering their brown gills. Many chefs, however, feel that cultivated mushrooms improve in flavor if they are a few days old. Buy 1 pound for 4 portions.

Prepare mushrooms by wiping them with a damp paper towel. Do not wash them unless they are very dirty. Trim the bottom of the stems. Leave small ones whole; slice or quarter larger ones. For baked or broiled mushroom caps, buy very large ones. Trim the stems even with the cap. If they are to be stuffed, remove the stem completely.

Steaming. Although mushrooms are usually sautéed, some recipes call for cooked mushrooms as a garnish. These should be steamed so they do not become brown. Clean medium-size mushrooms and leave them whole. In a heavy pan put 1 tablespoon lemon juice, 1 teaspoon salt and water to a 1/4-inch level. Bring to a boil and add the mushrooms. Cover the pan, lower the heat, and cook for about 5 minutes, shaking the pan so the mushrooms do not stick.

A butterless way of cooking sliced mushrooms is to heat a large skillet and sprinkle it with a teaspoon of salt. Add the sliced mushrooms; shake the pan and stir the mushrooms for a few minutes until they start to give up their juices. Add 2 tablespoons of water and continue to cook over lowered heat, while stirring, for about 2 minutes. Sprinkle with a few drops of lemon juice and serve.

Broiling. To broil mushrooms, remove stems, brush caps with butter or oil and broil them, cap up, 4 to 5 inches from the source of heat, for 3 to 4 minutes. Turn them over and put a dot of butter in each cap. Sprinkle with salt and pepper and broil for about 3 minutes. Serve them cap up.

Onions

Probably the most widely used vegetable, used raw or boiled, baked, roasted, fried or braised.

Bermuda onions are large and flat. Usually white, sometimes tan, they are mild and sweet for slicing raw. Spanish onions are large, yellow brown and sweet and mild. Good raw, they are often baked or stuffed and baked. Yellow onions are medium-size cooking onions with a strong flavor; 3 to 5 onions make a pound. White onions are small, about 20 to the pound, and are usually boiled and creamed or simmered in a stew. Red or Italian onions are usually served raw. They are often combined with cooked red cabbage. Other members of the onion family are green onions, called scallions or spring onions, leeks, shallots and garlic.

The easiest way to peel onions is to drop them into boiling water for 1 or 2 minutes. The skin will then slip off easily. When peeling onions, leave the root end on so that they retain their shape.

Parsnips

An unjustifiably neglected vegetable, parsnips have a sweet flavor that many are unfamiliar with. Look for roots with fat round tops, rather than long thin ones. Allow 2 1/2 pounds for 4 portions.

If serving parsnips puréed or simply sliced and buttered, peel them after they are cooked, as it is easier.

Boiling. Scrub parsnips well. Cook them in boiling salted water to cover for 5 to 15 minutes, depending on size. Do not cook them until they are soft and mushy. Plunge them into cold water to facilitate peeling.

Purée them in a food processor or food mill; sprinkle with 1 teaspoon each of salt and sugar and stir in 2 or 3 tablespoons of butter. Parsnips can be prepared ahead of time and held over hot water. Another way: top with bread crumbs, dot with butter, and bake in a 350°F oven for about 25 minutes. They can be served sliced, tossed with melted butter, salt and pepper. Also they are delicious roasted, and they can be baked with sliced potatoes.

Peas

Fresh peas are a truly delicious vegetable, but the season for them is short. Unfortunately, many of the fresh peas available are too old and they then become starchy. The best test is to open a pod and bite into a pea. The little tiny peas that the French call *petits pois* are readily available frozen and are very good. Do not, however, cook them at all. Simply pour boiling water over them or toss for a minute with melted butter, just long enough to heat them. A new pea on the market, called the sugar snap pea, has an edible pod. The peas in the pod are fully formed, which is different from the Chinese snow pea which is flat and has tiny embryo peas in its pod.

If you are shelling peas, allow 3 to 4 pounds for 4 servings; 1 pound will give you 1 cup shelled peas.

Boiling. Cook at a simmer in unsalted boiling water for about 10 minutes, or until tender. Add a few pea pods to the water for flavor.

Drain and toss with butter, salt and pepper. Sprinkle the peas with chopped fresh mint or tarragon or parsley. Toss them with pearl onions that have been boiled until barely tender. Combine them with sliced sautéed mushrooms.

Sugar snap peas should be stemmed and the strings removed. Cook in boiling unsalted water for only 1 to 2 minutes. Drain and toss with butter, salt and pepper. They can also be steamed for just a few minutes until they turn bright green.

Chinese snow peas are treated the same way as sugar snap peas. They should be cooked briefly so that they retain all their delicious crispness.

Peppers

A native of the Americas, peppers come in a wide variety, both sweet and hot, and are red, green, yellow and even purple. When buying peppers, look for bright firm skins. Avoid any that feel soft or are wrinkled. Purchase 1 pepper per person.

Boiling. Sweet peppers, red, green or yellow, are often stuffed and baked. The peppers should be parboiled first. Wash them well. Using a small knife, cut around the stem and lift off the top. Scoop out the ribs and seeds and discard them. Parboil the peppers in lightly salted boiling water to cover in a covered pan, for about 6 minutes. They should be crisp-tender. Remove from water and drain upside down on paper towels before stuffing.

Broiling. "Roasted" sweet pepper strips are often added to other vegetables for color and flavor. They are trimmed and then broiled, whole or

quartered, 2 inches from the source of heat. Turn them frequently for about 15 minutes until they are blackened and charred. Drop into a paper bag for about 5 minutes. The steam that collects helps loosen the skins. Use your fingers and the tip of a sharp knife to cut off the skins. Cut into strips or pieces of whatever size the recipe calls for.

Potatoes

One of the most important vegetables in our diet, the potato is native to the Andes of South America and was brought to Europe by the *conquistadores.* It is cooked by boiling, steaming, baking, roasting and frying.

Different kinds of potatoes are best suited for certain methods of cooking. The Idaho or baking potato is best for baking, and it can be used in some casseroles, or can be boiled for mashing. The all-purpose potato, sometimes called the Maine potato, is best for boiling and roasting. New potatoes can be red or white. They are often dyed to accentuate the redness. They are delicious steamed. Allow 2 pounds for 4 portions. For baking potatoes, allow 1 potato for each person. If very large, one will serve 2 persons.

When buying potatoes pick firm, well-shaped ones and reject any that are soft, green-tinged, blemished, or are sprouting "eyes."

Boiling. Scrub potatoes well. Peel them or leave the skins on. They hold their shape better for slicing if unpeeled. Place in boiling salted water and cook, covered, for 25 to 30 minutes, or until tender when pierced with a knife. Drain, return to the pan over low heat, and shake briskly to evaporate moisture. Peel and serve hot with butter, salt and pepper.

Steaming. A delicious way to prepare tiny new potatoes. Wash well and cut off a strip of skin around the middle of the potato. Place in a steamer over boiling salted water, cover, and cook for 10 to 20 minutes, or more, depending on the size.

Serve boiled or steamed potatoes

tossed with parsley or herb butter. Combine 4 tablespoons melted butter with 4 tablespoons minced parsley or a combination of parsley with mint or basil.

Baking. Scrub baking potatoes well and either pierce with a fork or make a 1/2-inch slit in the skin with a knife. This prevents the potato's bursting in the heat of the oven. If you like a soft skin, rub it with butter or oil. Cooking in foil will keep the skin soft, but foil-cooked potatoes will be moist inside rather than the usual dry potato texture. Bake in a preheated 375°F oven for about 1 hour. An aluminum nail inserted into a potato will shorten the cooking time. If you bake at a higher temperature, such as 425°F, they will bake more quickly.

Cut an X into the top of the baked potato, or simply slit it, and squeeze to loosen the contents. Serve with butter, salt and pepper, or top with sour cream or cottage cheese and chives. Add minced chives, dill, basil or parsley to melted butter and serve on the potatoes. Bacon bits are often added to baked potatoes.

Spinach

Available all year round, often prewashed and packed in plastic, this is a delicious and versatile vegetable. If your market has loose spinach, you will find it worth the extra work of washing as you can pick leaves that are dark green and fresh. It must be rinsed very well, best in lukewarm water, and coarse stems should be discarded.

Spinach can be served raw in a salad, but it is delicious as a cooked vegetable. Buy 2 to 2 1/2 pounds for 4 portions.

Steaming. Put washed spinach in a large pan; do not add any water. Cover the pan and steam spinach in its own juices, turning it several times with wooden spoons, for 6 to 8 minutes. Drain spinach and serve with butter, salt and pepper. For added flavor, add a pinch of freshly ground nutmeg.

Variation: Remove the spinach after about 5 minutes and drain it. Chop it, either coarse or fine, and reheat it with

Roasting Potatoes

1 Place butter or rendered chicken, beef or goose fat in an ovenproof dish in 425°F oven.

2 Parboil potatoes in boiling salted water for 10 minutes, Peel; cut large ones into halves or quarters.

3 Potato pieces can be dusted with flour.

OR For a decorative, crisp finish, scratch the surface of the potatoes with a fork.

4 When fat is sizzling but not smoking, remove pan from oven. Place potatoes in the fat.

5 Turn the potatoes with 2 spoons so that all sides are well coated with fat. Add any herbs.

OR Place the potatoes around the meat in pan base when the fat has started to run. Turn in fat.

6 Baste the potatoes from time to time during cooking. Turn them once with 2 spoons.

7 When the potatoes are brown on the outside, remove from the dish and serve. Discard herbs.

some heavy cream, salt, pepper and nutmeg. Creamed spinach can also be used as a base for poached eggs or fish. Top with a Mornay sauce and grated cheese, and finish under the broiler.

Squash

There are many species of this native American vegetable. The various kinds are usually divided into summer squash and winter squash.

Summer squash are yellow squash, both crookneck and straightneck (fatter), 2 to 4 per pound. Pattypan, or cymling, is flat and round with a scalloped edge. Zucchini, sometimes called by their French name, *courgettes,* are a summer squash but are now available most of the year. Sometimes called Italian squash, these have dark green skin. All of these can be steamed, baked, sautéed or boiled.

Winter squash are usually baked or boiled and mashed.

Allow 2 pounds of any squash for 4 portions.

Summer Squash

Wash well. Zucchini do not need to be peeled. Some yellow squashes may need to be peeled. Slice crosswise. Cymlings can be quartered if small, and cubed if large; or can be left whole for stuffing.

Boiling. Place the prepared squash in a small amount of boiling salted water, cover the pan, and cook until they are just crisp-tender, anywhere from 6 to 15 minutes, depending on size and type. Do not let them get soggy. Drain well.

Toss with a little butter, pepper and perhaps a dash of lemon juice, or toss with tomato sauce and sprinkle with grated Parmesan cheese. Combine with an equal amount of cooked sliced carrots and toss with butter and a teaspoon of chopped fresh mint or basil. Cook with chopped scallions.

Winter Squash

Winter squash, such as acorn or Hubbard, is usually split lengthwise and seeded. If the squash half does not sit flat, balance it on a ring of crumbled foil. Do not trim squash pieces on the bottom as juices will escape and burn on the pan. Place them, cut side up, on a baking sheet.

Baking. To bake in foil, place each half on a large piece of heavy-duty foil. Sprinkle with salt and pepper and dot with butter. Wrap tightly. Place the foil packages on a baking sheet in a preheated 375°F oven and bake for about 45 minutes, or until tender.

Sweet Potatoes and Yams

The sweet potato, sometimes called the Jersey, is smaller and fluffier than the yam. It has yellow flesh. The yam is orange-colored and less dry. The two can be used interchangeably. They can be baked, boiled and roasted. Allow 1 sweet potato per person.

Baking. Wash and scrub potatoes and bake in a 400°F oven for 35 minutes to 1 hour, until potatoes are somewhat soft to the touch; use a potholder or towel to test.

Boiling. Wash the potatoes and cut off the tips. Do not peel. Cook in boiling salted water in a covered pan for 35 to 40 minutes, or until just tender. Drain and serve with butter, salt and pepper. Boiled potatoes can also be peeled and mashed with butter.

Oven Roasting. Arrange slices of peeled potatoes in a buttered baking dish. Sprinkle with ½ cup sugar and dot with butter. Add a little salt and bake at 375°F until potatoes are glazed and browned lightly.

Tomatoes

The tomato, or love apple, was once considered poisonous and was grown for decorative purposes. Unfortunately, today's tomatoes are not always very tempting; for many recipes, canned plum tomatoes, sometimes called Italian or egg tomatoes, are recommended for flavor.

If you are lucky enough to get garden-fresh tomatoes which need a bit more ripening, place them in a perforated bag along with a ripe apple and put in a cool place.

Peel tomatoes by plunging into boiling water for 30 seconds. Place in cold water, peel and core.

Broiling. Tomatoes for broiling are not peeled. Slice off the top, squeeze slightly and turn over on paper towels to drain. Preheat the broiler; arrange tomatoes on a lightly greased broiling pan. Dot with butter or brush with oil. Sprinkle with salt and pepper. Broil about 5 inches from the source of heat for 10 minutes.

Variations: Rub a slice of bread with garlic and grate or blend to make bread crumbs. Mix with oil and spread on tomatoes before broiling. Or top with grated or shredded cheese and broil only until cheese is bubbly and browned, about 4 minutes. Garnish with chopped parsley.

Turnips

The turnip family includes the small round white one with a purple band as well as the very large, yellow-fleshed rutabaga, or Swede, as it is often called. White turnips are peeled and sliced or cubed, either for cooking or for adding raw to a salad.

Boiling. Turnips can be boiled in salted water or beef or chicken stock for 15 to 20 minutes, until just tender. Drain and serve with butter, salt and pepper.

Roasting. Turnips take on a wonderful flavor when roasted in the juices of a pork roast or ham. For roasting, cut the turnips into large cubes. They can also be roasted without meat and in combination with other vegetables.

Boiling. The large rutabaga, or Swede, must be peeled very well; the skin is often waxed. Cut into slices or cubes. Boil in salted water for 20 to 30 minutes. Drain well and mash. Reheat mashed turnip to evaporate excess moisture; add butter and salt and pepper to taste.

Baked Acorn Squash

4 portions

2	acorn squash, about 1 pound each
1	teaspoon salt

4	tablespoons unsalted butter

Wash the squash and split them lengthwise. Remove all seeds and fibers (seeds are good for birdfood). Set the halves, cut sides down, in a large baking dish containing ½ inch of water. Slide the pan into a preheated 350°F oven and bake the squash for 30 minutes. Most of the water will have evaporated.

Use tongs or potholders to turn the squash halves cut side up. Sprinkle each one with ¼ teaspoon salt and drop 1 tablespoon butter into the hollow. Continue to bake for 20 minutes longer, or until squash is as tender as you like. From time to time spoon up the butter in the hollow and trickle it over the cut surface, so the top does not dry out. Add no sweetening, no spices; just let the natural sweet taste of the golden vegetable be revealed.

Asparagus in Cream

6 portions

2	pounds asparagus
2	shallots
	salt

2	tablespoons butter
1	tablespoon lemon juice
½	cup heavy cream

Wash asparagus, remove scales, snap off the tough bottom ends, and peel the stalks. Cut each stalk across into pieces as long as the stalk is wide; the pieces should be about the size of large peas. Peel and mince the shallots. Put the asparagus pieces in a saucepan, sprinkle with 1 teaspoon salt, just cover with water, and bring to a boil. Cook uncovered for 4 minutes, then drain in a colander, rinse with cold water, and drain again.

Melt the butter in the same saucepan and add the minced shallots. Sauté over moderate heat until shallots are translucent. Turn in the drained asparagus and add the lemon juice. Stir gently to coat all the asparagus pieces with butter. Pour in the cream and simmer, stirring occasionally, until asparagus is fully cooked and the cream slightly thickened. Serve as is, or on toast.

Indian Beans

4 portions

1 pound green snap beans
1 small onion
1 teaspoon fresh
  gingerroot
2 tablespoons butter

3 tablespoons water
pinch of ground fennel
  seed
salt

Prepare beans for cooking; chop the onion and grate the gingerroot. Place the butter and the water in a heavy pan with a close-fitting lid and bring to a boil. Add the beans, onion, gingerroot and fennel seed, and mix well. Cover the pan, lower heat slightly, and cook for 7 to 8 minutes, shaking the pan from time to time. Season to taste.

Beans Italian Style

4 portions

1 pound green or wax beans
1½ cups canned plum
  tomatoes
½ cup beef stock

1 teaspoon salt
⅛ teaspoon black pepper
1 tablespoon minced parsley

Prepare beans for cooking. Place the beans in a large heavy skillet with a cover. Drain tomatoes and reserve the juice. Add the tomatoes, breaking them up with a wooden spoon. Pour in stock and add salt and pepper. Add some of reserved tomato juice. Cover and simmer for 20 to 25 minutes, until beans are just tender. Add parsley. Serve beans with the pan juices.

Variations: Serve with grated Parmesan cheese. Instead of beef stock, use all the liquid from the tomatoes; increase the salt and add a pinch of basil.

Red Cabbage with Caraway

4 portions

1 medium-size red onion
1 pound red cabbage
1 or 2 garlic cloves
1 large green apple
3 tablespoons butter or
  cooking oil
4 tablespoons red wine or
  red-wine vinegar

2 teaspoons caraway seeds
½ teaspoon salt
¼ teaspoon black pepper
1 tablespoon sugar
1 bay leaf
minced fresh parsley

Peel and slice the onion and finely shred the cabbage. There should be about 4 cups of cabbage. Peel garlic and put through a press. Wash, peel, and core the apple, and grate it.

In a large heavy pan with a tight-fitting lid, sauté the onion and garlic in the butter or oil. When tender, add the cabbage and everything else except the parsley. Toss and mix well. Cover the pan and cook over moderately high heat for about 10 minutes. Toss occasionally during the cooking; add a little water if necessary. If liquid has not evaporated, turn up heat and boil, uncovered, to evaporate any excess. Transfer to a hot serving dish. Garnish with parsley.

Cauliflower with Salami and Tomatoes

4 portions

1 cauliflower	8 ounces ripe tomatoes
salt	8 very thin slices of salami
5 tablespoons butter	pepper
¼ cup bread crumbs	¼ cup grated cheese

Trim and core the cauliflower and divide into florets. Cook in about 1 inch of boiling salted water in a covered pan over moderate heat for 8 to 10 minutes. Drain thoroughly. Melt 1 tablespoon butter in a small pan and lightly brown the bread crumbs. Slice the tomatoes. Preheat broiler.

Butter a gratin dish with 1 tablespoon of the butter, and arrange the florets in the dish. Remove rind from salami and tuck folded slices in between the florets. Season with pepper. Arrange slices of tomatoes on top of the cauliflower. Combine the grated cheese with the bread crumbs and spread on top of the tomatoes. Dot the top with remaining butter. Broil until hot, bubbling and crisp on top.

Variations: Substitute thin slices of cooked sausage or ham for the salami.

Purée the cooked florets, spread in a buttered gratin dish, and top with bread crumbs and cheese. Dot with butter and brown lightly.

Peas with Onions

4 portions

3	pounds fresh small green peas	2	shallots
1	teaspoon sugar	4	green onions (scallions)
1	teaspoon salt	4	tablespoons butter
12	ounces small white onions (silverskins)	¼	teaspoon black pepper

Shell the peas; there should be 3 cups. Rinse them, and place in a saucepan. Sprinkle peas with the sugar and ½ teaspoon salt and pour in enough hot water to cover the peas. Bring to a boil and cook the peas for 4 to 10 minutes, depending on the size and natural tenderness. Taste one to be sure when they are nearly but not quite done. Drain in a colander, rinse with very cold water, and drain again.

While the peas are cooking, put the white onions in a saucepan, cover with boiling water, and boil for about 5 minutes. Pour into a colander, then pour the onions into a bowl of cold water. Take them out one by one and peel them: cut off the root ends and pop them out of their skins. Halve the onions.

Blanch the shallots and the scallions in boiling water for 1 minute and drain. Peel shallots and cut into thin slices. Trim scallions and cut into ¼-inch crosswise slices.

Melt the butter in a saucepan over moderate heat and add onions, shallots and scallions. Cook, stirring frequently, for 8 to 10 minutes, until onions are golden and tender; test with a skewer to be sure. Stir in the peas and sprinkle in the pepper and remaining salt. Simmer over low heat for 3 to 4 minutes, until peas are completely tender. Spoon the vegetables into a warmed serving dish.

Variation: When fresh peas and small onions are not available, use 3 cups frozen *petits pois* and 8 ounces frozen peeled pearl onions.

New Peas with Cream

4 portions

2	pounds fresh peas in pods	1	teaspoon salt
1	small green onion (scallion)	1	tablespoon butter
1	teaspoon sugar	¼	cup light cream
		¼	teaspoon pepper

Shell peas; keep half of the pods and wash and drain them. Trim and chop the green onion. Place peas, sugar, salt, pea pods and chopped scallion in a heavy saucepan. Add enough boiling water to cover. Cover the pan and cook over moderate heat for 10 to 15 minutes, until just tender. The liquid should be almost evaporated. Drain, discard pea pods, and return peas to the pan.

Add butter and let it melt over low heat. Add cream and pepper. Leave over heat only long enough to heat the cream. Serve immediately.

Variations: Cook 2 or 3 fresh mint leaves with the peas. Add 6 tiny new potatoes, cooked and peeled, to the peas before adding the cream. Mix sautéed mushrooms with the peas before adding the cream.

Baked Onions au Gratin

6 portions

	butter for baking dish	½	cup chicken or beef stock
12	onions, each 3 ounces	½	cup grated Cheddar cheese
	salt and pepper		

Butter a 9- or 10-inch ovenproof dish. Peel the onions and place them in the buttered dish. Sprinkle with salt and pepper and pour in the stock. Cover and bake in the center of a preheated 325°F oven for about 1 hour, or until tender. Add more stock if necessary.

Cover the top with grated cheese and place under the broiler for a few minutes, until the cheese is melted.

Variation: Substitute ½ cup thin tomato juice for the stock.

Boiled Onions with Grated Cheese

4 to 6 portions

1½	pounds small white onions	6	tablespoons grated Cheddar cheese
3	tablespoons butter	1	tablespoon minced fresh parsley
1	teaspoon salt		

Cut a cross in the root end of each onion. Put the unpeeled onions in a large saucepan, cover with water, and bring to a boil. Simmer for 8 to 10 minutes, until an onion pierced with a skewer tests done. Pour onions into a colander, rinse with cold water, and drain. Peel the onions as soon as they are cool enough to handle.

Have ready a shallow, flameproof, 4-cup gratin dish. Melt the butter in the dish, then add the peeled onions and sprinkle them with salt. Set the dish over low heat, over an asbestos pad if necessary to maintain low heat, and gently warm the onions, turning them with a wooden spoon. When they begin to look gilded, sprinkle the cheese on top, cover the dish with a sheet of foil, and leave over the low heat for 2 minutes, until the cheese is melted. Remove foil, sprinkle the cheese with parsley, and serve from the dish.

Polonaise Topping

(for Brussels sprouts, cauliflower or asparagus)

2 hard-cooked eggs	⅔ cup fresh white bread
2 tablespoons chopped	crumbs
parsley	1 teaspoon freshly ground
3 tablespoons butter	black pepper
	1 teaspoon salt

Shell and chop the eggs. Combine chopped eggs and parsley in a small bowl. Melt the butter in a small saucepan over moderate heat. Add the bread crumbs and cook slowly, stirring, for about 10 minutes until crumbs are golden. Add pepper and salt to the chopped egg and parsley and sprinkle on top of the cooked vegetable. Top with browned bread crumbs and serve at once.

Three-Vegetable Mélange

6 portions

3 small white turnips, 3	2 zucchini, about 6 ounces
ounces each	each
4 medium-size carrots, 3	3 tablespoons butter
ounces each	salt and pepper

Wash and peel turnips and cut into julienne strips. Scrub and scrape carrots and cut into julienne strips. Scrub zucchini but do not peel. Cut into julienne strips. There should be 2 cups of each vegetable. Blanch turnip and carrot strips in boiling salted water for 1 minute. Drain and plunge into cold water. This may be done in advance.

When ready to serve, melt the butter in a heavy sauté pan or skillet with a cover. Add zucchini strips and cook for 1 minute. Add carrots and turnips, mix well and cover the pan. Cook for about 2 minutes and check; vegetables should be hot and crisp-tender. Season with salt and pepper. Serve immediately.

Variations: Try other vegetable combinations: parsnips, peeled broccoli stems, etc.

Potatoes Montrouge

4 to 6 portions

4 medium-size potatoes
4 to 6 medium-size carrots
1 egg
4 tablespoons grated
   Cheddar or Parmesan or
   Gruyère cheese

2 tablespoons butter, melted
2 tablespoons sour cream or
   yogurt
   salt and pepper
   butter and cheese for top
   (optional)

Scrub potatoes and carrots and cook them in boiling salted water until tender. Peel them and mash thoroughly. Combine the potatoes and carrots. Beat the egg with the cheese, melted butter, sour cream or yogurt, and salt and pepper to taste. Combine egg mixture with carrots and potatoes and place vegetables in an ovenproof serving dish. Dot the top with a little butter and sprinkle on a bit more cheese. Place under the broiler until top is browned.

Sunchokes Avgolemono

4 portions

1 pound sunchokes
  juice of 3 lemons
½ cup chicken stock

2 egg yolks
1 tablespoon chopped fresh
  parsley

Scrub sunchokes carefully, then drop into a pan of boiling water with the juice of 1 lemon. Simmer for 8 minutes. Drain, rinse with cold water, and let them cool until they can be handled. Peel the sunchokes and cut them into ¼-inch-thick slices. Test the vegetables; if they are completely tender, go on with the recipe; if they are still hard in the center, cover again with boiling water and simmer for 2 minutes longer. Pour off the cooking liquid and replace it with the chicken stock. Slowly bring it to a simmer. Meanwhile, beat remaining lemon juice with the egg yolks and pour the mixture into the sunchokes, stirring as you do, to mix well. As soon as all the egg mixture is poured in, remove the pan from the heat, but continue stirring gently until the liquid is thickened. Do not stir vigorously, lest the sunchokes break up. Spoon into a serving bowl and sprinkle with parsley.

Part Four
PUFF PASTRY

Puff pastry, or *pâte feuilletée,* is one of the eight classic French pastry doughs listed in the *Larousse Gastronomique,* and is one of the most ethereal and delicious products of the repertoire of the *pâtissier.*

Most people believe that this buttery pastry dough is so difficult to make properly that it is impossible for a nonprofessional even to attempt it. This is not true. Although there are many popular misconceptions about this dough, it is one that deserves to be better understood and appreciated by American cooks. The processes involved in making puff pastry are simple, taken one at a time, and the results are extremely rewarding.

Pâte feuilletée, or puff paste, is best known to us as the crisp, flaky dough used to make the luscious pastries called Napoleons. This pastry, called *mille-feuilles* (a thousand leaves) in France, was known at least as far back as the sixteenth century. Carême may have used it for some of the elaborate pastry pieces that adorned his banquet tables. This pastry is not called a Napoleon in honor of the emperor but more probably as a corruption of *Napolitain,* referring to the Neapolitan style of layering pastry sweets and ices in alternating bands of texture and color.

The dough gets its name from the way it is prepared and baked. Butter is enclosed within a simple pastry dough, and the resulting parcel is rolled and folded numerous times. Each time the pastry is rolled out and folded is called a "turn." As the dough receives at least six turns, the number of layers—alternating sheets of dough and butter—increases geometrically. Four single turns, for example, produce nearly 250 layers of dough and butter.

As the pastry is baked in a hot oven, it rises. However, because the butter has been "rolled in," the pastry rises in separate layers, rather than as a solid mass. This occurs because the moisture in the butter is released as steam, causing the upper layers to rise; this traps air between the layers. The result—hundreds of buttery flakes, or "leaves."

There are two key factors for success: Everything must be consistently and constantly cold—the butter, the dough, the pastry maker's hands. The technique of rolling the dough in a series of repeated rollings and folds must be performed quickly and with dispatch, until the dough becomes increasingly smooth, glossy and easy to handle with each turn. Modern refrigeration is an invaluable ally to the home pastry chef because the dough can be repeatedly cooled to the proper temperature before the next rolling and folding.

The origins of puff pastry are not known, and it is intriguing to surmise how the inventor even suspected that butter incorporated in the dough in this way would lead to such spectacular results.

Some culinary historians credit the ancient Persians with making the first type of puff pastry, and there are indeed many recipes for savory little pies called *borek,* and many dessert specialties in the cuisines of the Middle East that call for the use of a similar pastry. Following this historical thread, the Persians must have passed on their recipes for puff pastry to the Greeks, whose cuisine also includes many specialties based on it.

According to *The Horizon Cookbook,* "In medieval France *gâteaux feuilletés* were so popular that Robert, Bishop of Amiens, mentioned them in a charter of 1311, but it was not until the seventeenth century that the arduous process of making puff pastry was simplified, probably by Claude Lorrain, an erstwhile *pâtissier* before becoming a landscape painter."

Some sources claim that a pastry cook named Feuillet invented puff pastry, especially since his name seems to be related. Carême himself said that he admired Feuillet, and in the esteemed *Dictionnaire Universel de Cuisine,* Joseph Favre credits Feuillet as the inventor of puff pastry.

In 1655 François La Varenne published the first comprehensive French cookbook on pastry making, called *Le Pastissier François.* According to Anne Willan, ". . . few copies survive, no doubt because of the sticky fingers of the loyal craftsmen who have used it over the years. And no wonder; many modern cookbooks could take a lesson from *Le Pastissier,* with its step-by-step directions, accurate measurements and instructions for

temperature control . . . The methods in *Le Pastissier* for making pie pastry, puff pastry, macaroons, and waffles, for instance, are precisely the same today . . ." *(Great Cooks and Their Recipes).*

The perfect execution of this pastry is one of the key reasons for the preeminence of French pastry in the world today. However, because the repeated rolling and folding (turns) of the dough must be executed with care while maintaining a constant control over the temperature of the dough and butter, people assume the job is too arduous and time-consuming for the home cook. However, Carême wrote in his classic work *Le Pâtissier Royal Parisien,* that he believed only twenty minutes were needed to prepare puff pastry, and he went on to criticize his colleagues who demanded longer.

The dough for puff pastry consists of two parts: the initial dough mixture, or *détrempe,* and the butter. Carême called the *détrempe,* which means watered down, "the soul of the operation." Before going on to detail recipes for several pastries, Carême gave numerous tips for making the pastry, including procedural differences for summer and winter baking, and the advice that the same man should make and bake the dough. It is important that the dough and the butter be of the same consistency and at similar temperatures for even layering; the dough is usually chilled between folds.

Once you have puff pastry on hand, its uses are limitless for both sweet and savory dishes. The dough is shaped to take advantage of its rising powers, so that as it bakes, it puffs into characteristic shapes such as cream horns or palm-leaf cookies. The crisp lightness of this pastry makes it an ideal choice for hot hors d'oeuvres in various guises. The *Larousse Gastronomique* with its lengthy entry on "Hors d'Oeuvre" mentions many uses for puff pastry, with each category followed by several compatible fillings: *allumettes* (matchsticks), *barquettes* (small boat-shaped tarts), *bouchées* ("mouthfuls," or tiny patty shells), *cannelons* (filled rectangles), *cornets* (horns), *talmouses* (dumplings with corners pinched at the top), and *tartelettes* (tiny round tarts). Other varieties include savory croissants, rolls and wafers.

Savory items baked *en croûte,* such as beef Wellington, have always been regarded as magnificent *pièces de résistance.* But equally impressive, although somewhat more delicate, are such lighter items as filled appetizer *feuilletés,* rectangles of pastry filled with fresh asparagus or seafood, bathed in a buttery sauce. Some enterprising *nouvelle cuisine* chefs have concocted savory appetizer versions of familiar dessert pastries, such as *mille-feuilles* of salmon.

Dessert pastries are the principal use for *pâte feuilletée,* and the most familiar classics are the *mille-feuilles* and simple fruit tarts. A *jalousie* is a lattice-topped fruit tart, and the *gâteau Pithiviers,* named after the town of its origin, is a large round pastry filled with a rich almond cream. Similar items include *galettes,* or wafers, and *chaussons,* or rough turnovers.

Smaller pastries made with puff pastry, actually considered cookies or *petits fours,* include such items as *arcs, croissants, palmiers* and *papillons* (the traditional palm-leaf and butterfly shapes), *dartois, allumettes glacées* (frosted matchsticks), *cornets* (such as cream horns), *rouleaux* (rolls), and *sacristains* (twisted almond strips).

Because puff pastry freezes extremely well, today's home cook can make this versatile pastry at a leisurely pace and have it conveniently on hand to create impressive and delicious pastry masterpieces at a moment's notice.

PUFF PASTRY

Three types of pastry puff up into crisp, tender layers during baking: classic puff pastry; rough or quick puff pastry; and flaky pastry. All three are composed of alternate layers of dough and fat, created by rolling and folding the dough, a process referred to as "turns." Puff pastry in French is *pâte feuilletée,* which means pastry of many leaves.

Classic Puff Pastry

This pastry results in the most even layering, crispest and flakiest texture. It uses equal weight of butter and flour and is the most time-consuming to produce because it must be allowed to rest or "relax" for 30 minutes to 1 hour between turns. The basic technique involves mixing a very small amount of the flour with most of the butter to form a square package. The remainder of the butter is mixed with the bulk of the flour to form a dough which is wrapped around the butter package. The dough is then rolled and folded, usually 6 turns, thus creating 729 layers.

Puff Pastry

makes 1 pound

8 ounces (2 cups)
  all-purpose flour
1 teaspoon salt
1 tablespoon lemon juice
8 ounces unsalted butter

1 Sift the flour and salt into a bowl and place in the refrigerator to chill. Make ice water and measure out 6 tablespoons.

2 Make well in the flour. Add half the water and all the juice. Beat in some flour with fingers, until mixture is like thick cream. Add rest of water. Beat in rest of flour.

6 Place butter lengthwise in center of the circle. Lift dough at the long sides over the butter to overlap. Press gently with rolling pin to seal.

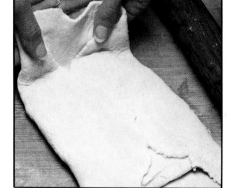

7 Lift short edges over and press the same way. You will now have a rectangle of pastry. If it looks misshapen, push into shape with a knife.

8 Turn rectangle so that long sides face you. Rolling in one direction with light pressure, roll out until pastry is twice its size. Rest for 10 minutes.

Quick Puff Pastry

This pastry is less light but slightly more tender than classic puff pastry because it is made by first mixing all of the flour with all of the butter, or butter and fat, which is first cut into small lumps; then giving the dough 2 to 3 turns, thus creating 27 layers. The pastry uses a greater proportion of flour to butter (1⅓ to 1) than does classic puff pastry. Because it does not need to be rested until after the second turn, it is speedy to produce and is usually known as quick puff pastry.

Flaky Pastry

This is made by a combination of the two previous techniques. It is similar in texture to quick puff pastry but slightly less light. It uses only 2 parts butter to 3 parts flour. A small amount of the butter is mixed with the flour to form a dough. The remainder of the butter is layered into the dough between the folds in 3 parts or turns, thus creating 27 layers. It needs to relax for only about 15 minutes between turns, making it almost as speedy to produce as quick puff pastry and somewhat neater and easier to roll.

All three pastries are more refined and elegant than the standard short-crust pastry and serve to elevate a simple dish to something more special.

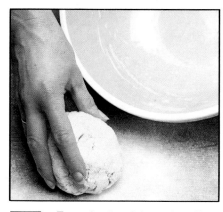

3 Form the dough into a ball. Turn onto a lightly floured surface and knead lightly 3 or 4 times. Wrap in wax paper and a damp cloth. Chill for 30 minutes.

4 Using a spatula, work the fat until it is of spreadable consistency. Spread on a sheet of wax paper to make a rectangle 4 × 6 inches. Chill.

5 Unwrap chilled dough and lightly flour a working surface. Roll out dough to a circle 12 inches in diameter. Peel paper away from rectangle of chilled butter.

9 Fold bottom third of pastry up and lower third down on top of it. Seal all edges lightly. Wrap in wax paper and a damp cloth. Rest for 15 minutes.

10 Pastry has had one rolling. Unwrap pastry. Fold should be on your left, longest sealed edge on your right. Roll and fold as before. Let rest for 30-60 minutes.

11 Repeat this operation at least three more times. Wrap loosely in plastic wrap and refrigerate at least two hours before use.

The pastry is ideal for covering pies, making a great variety of tarts and turnovers, and particularly for *en croûte* presentations (in a crust) such as the classic beef Wellington, coulibiac, whole striped bass and saucisson (sausage) en croûte.

Ingredients for Pastry

Light, flaky, rich pastry is dependent on air, water, fat and flour. Weighing the ingredients is the most accurate method but careful measuring works well too.

Flour. Unbleached, all-purpose flour is recommended for all flaky pastries because it contains a high percentage of hard wheat. The gluten found in hard wheat plays an important role in the pastry's ability to puff. Gluten, when activated by liquid and manipulation (kneading), contributes strength and structure to the dough. Gluten is made up of 1 part protein and 2 parts water. On heating, the water turns to steam, thus creating a great deal of pressure within the gluten structure, causing it to rise.

Fat. Margarine or butter can be used, or a mixture of the two. Margarine is easier to work with, as it softens less quickly and produces the best texture and rise, but the flavor of butter is incomparable. Correct proportions are essential: too much makes the pastry difficult to work with; too little and the pastry will be tough. The fat must be chilled or it will not disperse well to create layers and the pastry will stick, forcing the addition of more flour which would toughen the pastry.

Water, Lemon and Salt. Too much water will overactivate the gluten in the flour and toughen the pastry. Lemon juice, about 1 tablespoon, is sometimes used because it relaxes the gluten, making the pastry easier to roll out.

Pastry with a high butter content is best made in a cool area. Marble is the ideal surface for rolling the dough but any kitchen surface is fine if it is cool. If the dough starts to soften and stick, slip it onto a baking sheet and refrigerate until firm.

Shaping Puff Pastry

1 BOUCHÉES: Roll out the pastry to ¼-inch thickness. Dip a 1½-inch cutter into flour. Cut out a circle of pastry.

2 Using a small cutter or glass, mark a small circle in the center. Brush with beaten egg before baking.

1 MILLE-FEUILLES: For a large one, use half the basic recipe. Divide pastry into 3 pieces. Roll each to a strip 4 × 8 inches.

2 For a small one, divide into 3 pieces. Roll into strips. Divide each strip into 6 pieces. Brush tops of 6 pieces with beaten egg.

Pastry or baking sheets should be heavy for even heat distribution. Black metal or nonstick types are not suitable. Spraying sheets with water helps to prevent shrinking of pastry and creates additional steam to help the pastry rise. There is no need to grease the sheet as the butter content of the pastry is high enough to prevent it sticking.

A sharp knife or pizza cutter is essential for cutting uncooked pastry, as a clean cut ensures an unhindered rise. A rounded-blade metal spatula is useful for cutting the butter and for notching or scoring the shaped pastry.

Making superb flaky pastries does not require a strict adherence to a vast set of complicated rules and regulations. The secret lies in learning the art of correct handling. Heavy handling inevitably means a heavy pastry. Light handling with cool hands results in a pastry that is crisp, flaky and tender.

You do not need to have a marble slab and icy-cold hands to make flaky pastry, but keep calm and cool both physically and mentally. Have all your ingredients and equipment ready before you start because you should avoid stopping once you have begun to make the pastry. Chilling the equipment in the refrigerator and rinsing

1 VOL-AU-VENT: Use the same technique, but use a larger cutter and roll the pastry to ½-inch thickness.

2 For a large vol-au-vent, double the basic recipe and cut 2 circles 9 inches in diameter. Brush edge of one with beaten egg.

3 Cut a 7-inch lid from the other circle and place the border of pastry on the base. Press lightly. Bake lid separately.

1 TRANCHE: Roll out pastry to a rectangle 12 × 7 inches. Fold in half lengthwise.

2 Use a sharp knife to cut away a border of pastry 1½ inches wide. Set aside. Roll rectangle of pastry to the original size.

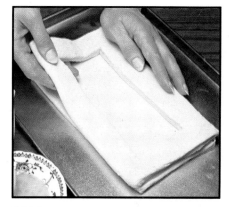

3 Brush edges of rectangle with beaten egg. Lift the border onto the edge. Press lightly to seal.

your hands under cold water make good sense. As already mentioned, it is essential to chill the fat.

Always give yourself plenty of time when making pastry and try to avoid fitting it in between other jobs. Perfect results require all your attention. Never try to hurry the processes along, especially if you are making a flaky pastry for the first time.

Allow at least 30 minutes for the pastry to relax before shaping and baking it. Wrap the pastry loosely in plastic wrap or a plastic bag and place it in the refrigerator.

If, at any time during the making,

the pastry or the fats get too warm, do not worry. Wrap the dough in plastic and refrigerate for up to 30 minutes before starting again. Never carry on regardless, hoping for the best.

Shaping

Once the pastry is in the refrigerator relaxing, you can justifiably feel happy with yourself, knowing that the major part of the job is over. All that remains to be done is the final rolling and shaping.

There are numerous ways to

shape flaky pastries, from triangular and round turnovers to fancy decorative envelopes and spectacular rolls.

Pastry dough is soft and tends to stretch easily, so it is necessary always to make sure that you and your baking equipment are well organized beforehand. Have ungreased baking sheets close at hand, to avoid carrying the cut shapes unneccessary distances. No greasing is needed for such buttery pastry, but it is important to dampen the baking sheets with water, which will vaporize in baking and keep the pastry from burning on the bottom.

Always roll the pastry with short

light strokes. When cutting, a sharp knife is essential. Make clean, decisive cuts, straight down, without dragging or stretching the pastry. A clean cut will ensure that the pastry rises with maximum expansion. In the process of cutting, the top of the piece will be pressed together; this might interfere with rising, therefore it is a good practice to place the cut pieces upside down on the baking sheet.

To transfer large pieces of rolled-out pastry, use an open-sided baking sheet, or gently roll pastry over a rolling pin and carefully lift and unroll over a pie or onto a baking sheet. To use pastry for a single-crust pie, follow the same technique as for short-crust pastry.

Baking

Flaky pastries require a hot oven in order to achieve the best rise and texture. The high heat causes the fats between the layers to melt. This leaves empty spaces where the steam and air expand to lift the layers of pastry and quickly set its structure into the final shape. If the pastry is placed in an oven that is not hot enough, the fat will melt and leak out before the starch in the flour has had time to absorb it. The resulting pastry will be dry, tough and heavy. Conversely, too hot an oven will set the surface of the pastry before it has had a chance to complete the rising.

Quick Puff Pastry

makes 1 pound

- 6 tablespoons lard
- 6 tablespoons butter
- 8 ounces (2 cups) all-purpose flour
- ½ teaspoon salt
- 6 tablespoons chilled water
- 2 teaspoons lemon juice

1 Cut fats into walnut-size pieces and place on a plate. Place plate in the refrigerator to keep fats chilled.

2 Sift flour and salt into a chilled bowl. Add chilled fats to flour and toss lightly with a thin spatula or table knife.

6 Place dough on board with length facing away from you. Lightly mark 3 equal sections across pastry with back of a knife.

7 Fold the section of dough nearest to you over the center, using both hands. Place the edge straight on the marked line.

8 Fold farthest section towards you so that it covers the other two. Seal pastry edges lightly with rolling pin or a finger.

Storing

Unbaked pastry keeps very well, if wrapped airtight and refrigerated, for up to 5 days; if frozen, it will keep for up to 6 months. Defrost frozen pastry in the refrigerator overnight, not at room temperature. Once baked, pastry is at its best if it is served the day it is made.

Warm pastry dishes should be eaten shortly after baking; holding them for any period of time will cause them to become soggy. To cool pastry, allow it to cool slowly, uncovered, in a draft-free area.

Puff Pastry

The lightest and finest of all the flaked pastries, puff pastry can be used for any recipe calling for flaky or quick puff pastry and for some special dishes where spectacular good looks are called for. Puff pastry made well has meltingly tender, paper-thin layers.

Used to make crisp, light cream cakes such as the classic *mille-feuilles* or delicious *vol-au-vents, bouchées* or pie toppings, it represents the peak of achievement for a pastry cook.

Despite its reputation as the thoroughbred of the pastry stable, puff pastry can be easy enough to make as long as you stick to the time-honored ritual and do not attempt shortcuts.

Before you begin, chill the ingredients. Sift the flour and salt into a bowl about 1 hour before you plan to make

3 Add water and lemon juice to bowl and carefully gather mixture together with fingertips to form a soft, pliable dough.

4 Turn dough out on a lightly floured board and shape by gently patting with fingertips. Do not knead.

5 Roll the dough with light short strokes, into a rectangle 15 × 5 inches. Do not overflour board or rolling pin.

9 Give dough a half turn so edges are top and bottom. Roll pastry to its original size and repeat folding and sealing.

10 Place pastry on a plate and cover with plastic wrap or a damp cloth. Place in refrigerator to relax for 30 minutes.

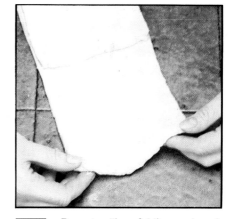

11 Repeat rolling, folding and sealing twice more. If the pastry is still mottled, roll and fold a fifth time. Relax for 30 minutes before shaping.

86
Flaky Pastry

makes 1 pound

6 tablespoons lard, chilled
6 tablespoons unsalted
   butter, chilled
8 ounces (2 cups)
   all-purpose flour
½ teaspoon salt
6 tablespoons ice water
2 teaspoons lemon juice
   (optional)

1 Divide each fat into 4 equal pieces and place 1 portion of each on 4 separate plates. Place 3 plates in refrigerator.

2 Sift flour and salt into bowl. Cut the first quarter of fats into flour. Add water and juice to make a soft nonsticky dough.

6 Fold fatless section of dough across center section, making sure edges of dough are straight. Brush off excess flour.

7 Carefully fold top section over center section, again making sure that edges of dough are straight. Brush off any flour.

8 Lightly seal the 3 raw edges with a rolling pin and press dough at intervals to distribute the air. Relax dough in refrigerator.

the pastry. Place the bowl in the refrigerator and leave it there until needed. Measure the water and refrigerate it as well. Measure the butter and leave it, covered, in the refrigerator until required. If your hands are inclined to be rather warm, keep a bowl of ice water handy so you can cool them from time to time.

Making the détrempe. To make the *détrempe,* or base dough, remove the bowl of chilled flour and the water from the refrigerator. Make a well in the

center of the flour and pour in about half of the water plus the lemon juice. Using your fingertips, gradually mix the flour into the water until the mixture in the well reaches the consistency of thick cream. Now add remaining liquid gradually, incorporating remaining flour as you go to make a firm dough. Turn this out onto a floured board and knead lightly until smooth.

Using your hands, flatten the pastry to a pad. Wrap this in wax paper, plastic wrap or a clean damp cloth and

leave in the refrigerator for 30 minutes. This will make the dough relax and will make it easier to manage when the time comes to incorporate the butter.

Preparing the butter. Unlike flaky pastry, where the fat is dotted over the basic dough, the butter for puff pastry is incorporated in a thin sheet. It is this that gives the pastry its characteristic layered appearance. To prepare the butter, put it on a large plate; using a spatula or a knife, work it until it is of a spreadable consistency. Have ready a

3 Turn out dough on a lightly floured surface; knead lightly. Pat dough into a rectangle; dust rolling pin with flour.

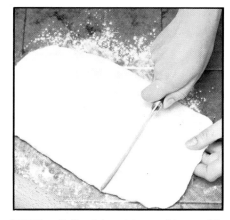

4 Roll out dough to an oblong, with short, light strokes. Use table knife to mark the dough lightly into 3 equal sections.

5 Cut another quarter of fats into small pieces and dot alternately over the top of 2 marked sections of dough.

9 Repeat process with second quarter of fats from refrigerator. Fold and roll to seal. Relax briefly, if time allows.

10 Repeat process with remaining fats. Fold and roll to seal. Relax dough again, if possible.

11 Relax the dough, covered in plastic wrap, in the refrigerator for 30 minutes before using.

sheet of wax paper. Spread the butter on the paper to make a rectangular pat measuring 4 × 6 inches. Cover with another sheet of wax paper and leave in the refrigerator for about 10 minutes.

Making the paton. Flour your chosen working surface very lightly, just enough to prevent the dough sticking. Also flour your rolling pin lightly. Roll out the *détrempe* to a circle 12 inches in diameter. Roll lightly, and from the center outwards. The trick when rolling puff pastry is to roll up and

away from you, then down towards you.

Gently peel the wax paper from the pat of butter. Place the butter lengthwise in the center of the circle of dough. The easiest way to do this is to lift the butter with a wide spatula.

Carefully lift the dough at the long sides of the butter rectangle and bring the sides over to cover the butter. The dough will overlap. Press down gently with the rolling pin to seal the edges. Do not thump or press hard; light

pressure will be enough. Bring the short ends over and seal in the same way. You now have a rectangle of pastry enclosing the butter, the *paton*. To achieve even layering, it is essential to keep the rectangle in a neat shape. Use the flat of a knife blade to push in the sides to make them even all around.

First rolling and folding. Rolling is the thing that can make or break your pastry. Get into the habit of rolling the pastry in one direction only. Use long, smooth, light strokes. Roll from the center going up and away from you, then down towards you; do not roll up, down and across. Roll just to the ends, not over them. This will keep the rectangle in shape; also rolling over the ends can push out the butter and destroy the layering.

Turn the *paton* so that the long sides face you. Roll out the package of dough and butter until it measures about twice its original size. If the pastry begins to become sticky or creamy, which indicates that the butter is softening too much, stop work and chill the package in the refrigerator for 10 minutes or so.

If the pastry is firm enough, or after it has chilled, fold up the bottom third of the dough and the upper third down on top of it. Seal all the edges lightly as before; wrap the pastry in wax paper and then in a clean damp cloth. The damp cloth will prevent a crust forming while the pastry rests. Allow the pastry to rest in the refrigerator for 15 minutes and make a note that it has had 1 rolling.

Second rolling and folding. Unwrap the pastry and lay it on a lightly floured surface so the fold is on your left-hand side and the longest sealed edge on your right. Roll out the pastry again to the same size as before and fold again as before. Wrap and rest again, making a note that this is the second rolling.

Final rolling, folding and resting. The pastry must be turned, rolled, folded and rested in this way another 4 times.

When you have completed the final rolling, wrap the pastry in plastic wrap and allow it to rest in the refrigerator for as long as possible. Overnight is best, but if you cannot manage this, aim for at least 2 hours.

Uses for Puff Pastry

Puff pastry can be used in a variety of ways.

Bouchées are tiny *vol-au-vents*, just enough to make a mouthful at a party. They should never be more than 1½ inches in diameter. *Bouchées* are simple to make; they are cut out with round cutters of the right size. Be sure the cutters are sharp, otherwise the pastry will be pulled out of shape at the edges. These are one of the shapes that should be placed upside down for baking.

Vol-au-vents are large versions of *bouchées*. You can make them 2 inches across for parties or 4 inches across to make a main course for 1 person. If you wish, you can make a container for a main course to serve 4 to 6 persons, by using double the recipe for puff pastry.

Mille-feuilles can be made large or small, sweet or savory. Large *mille-feuilles* can be served as a main course or as a dessert for 4 portions if you use half of the recipe for puff pastry. The same amount of pastry will make 10 to 12 small *mille-feuilles,* which you can fill with sweet or savory filling to serve as dessert cakes or light snacks.

A *tranche* is a long puff pastry container made by sticking a border of pastry onto a rectangle. *Tranches* can be filled with either sweet or savory mixtures. They are particularly good for sweet mixtures, as you can arrange fruit decoratively in them. The puff pastry recipe here makes a *tranche* to serve 8 to 10 portions.

Baking

Puff pastry for pastry cases should always be baked before it is filled, and it should never be filled until the last minute. Filling puff pastry too soon makes it soggy.

This pastry is always baked on a dampened, not greased, baking sheet in a 400°F oven. Greasing the baking sheet would make the bottom of the pastry fry. The time needed depends on what you are baking. When using the pastry as a pie topping or to wrap around meat, follow the recipe instructions carefully as these may vary the temperature to ensure that the filling is cooked.

Making Quick Puff Pastry

This pastry, also called rough puff pastry, rises in layers of flakes when baked just like the classic puff pastry. The quick version is easier and quicker to make. Flaky pastry and quick puff pastry contain the same proportions of ingredients, but the methods of preparation differ.

Quick puff pastry is the one to choose when you are looking for something special but do not have too much time to spare on the preparation. This is generally accepted as being the best pastry for dishes where the dough is to be shaped and decorated. It will hold its shape when baked and is therefore suitable for intricate decorations.

As is the case with classic puff pastry, when making the quick version all sorts of problems can occur if you allow the fats to become soft and sticky, as a result of stopping partway through the pastry making for any reason. The success of this pastry relies to a large extent on working with cold ingredients and equipment, quickly and efficiently, and on the fats being hard before you start. With quick puff pastry the fats should be taken straight from the refrigerator; they should be as hard as possible before they are added to the flour. Before you start, weigh or measure the fats, then cut them into walnut-size pieces and place on a plate. Return to the refrigerator to keep well chilled.

Adding the fats. Quick puff pastry, like all flaky pastries, depends on distributing the fats through the flour. The walnut-size pieces of fat are added to the sifted flour and salt all at once. The pieces are then tossed with flour to coat them.

Adding the liquid. Once the fats have been added to the flour, the next step is to add the water. Use chilled water, and measure it carefully; do not be tempted to add more than the stated amount. Too much liquid would give you an unmanageable dough. More seriously, it would result in a pastry that would harden on baking, showing no flaky layers from proper rising. Lemon juice is added with the water; chill both water and juice in the refrigerator.

The correct way to mix in the liquid is with a table knife or thin spatula. Again, a light hand is required so that none of the pieces of fat is broken down. More of a folding action is needed, so that the ingredients are bound together rather than stirred, creamed or rubbed in.

Forming the dough. Once the liquids are incorporated, the dough is ready to be quickly drawn together with the fingertips. The dough, once it has started to bind together, should not be kneaded into shape; all that is required is to gather it together with the fingertips.

Turn the dough out on a lightly floured board or surface. Avoid overflouring the surface or adding more flour to the dough even if it appears to be sticky. Pat the dough gently into a neat rectangle.

If the dough is sticky, place it on a lightly floured plate, cover with plastic wrap, and place in the refrigerator for about 20 minutes.

Rolling the dough. Roll the pastry with short, even strokes into a long rectangle approximately 15 × 5 inches. Avoid stretching the dough.

During this first rolling, take extra care to see that the side edges of the pastry are as neat and even as possible. Make sure, also, that the pastry is free

Palmiers

1 Sprinkle work surface with granulated sugar. Roll out pastry ¼ inch thick into a rectangle twice as long as it is wide.

2 Trim pastry edges so they are straight. Using the back of a knife, mark the pastry in the center across the width.

3 Roll over the pastry edge nearest to you, then, pushing with palms of both hands, roll it towards the marked line.

4 Turn pastry around and roll second half of pastry away from you so the second roll meets the first.

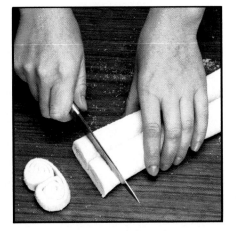

5 Using a small sharp knife, cut pastry rolls into ½-inch slices. Space the slices 1½ inches apart on a damp baking sheet.

6 Using the back of a large spoon, slightly flatten both sides of pastry slices, working from the center. Relax for 30 minutes before baking.

of excess flour. If there is any, brush it off gently with a pastry brush. The pastry at this point should have a mottled look. This shows that the fats are evenly distributed and your pastry is coming along successfully.

At this stage, the pieces of fat have formed mounds in the dough and it is these mounds of fat that melt to form cavities of air when the dough is baked. As the dough is subsequently

re-rolled several times, these raised knobs of fat are distributed through the dough, building up more and more potential cavities of air. This explains the need for the fats to be hard. If they were soft at this stage, the fats would be easily squashed, expelling any of the air that may have been built up.

Folding and sealing the dough. Once the dough has been rolled to the required length, it needs to be folded.

Lightly flour your hands and place the pastry with the length facing away from you. Lightly mark the dough with a table knife into 3 equal sections.

Lift the bottom section of the dough nearest to you and lay it over the center section, reaching the marked line. Do not press it down; just lay it on top, making sure that the raw edges are neatly aligned and not wavy. Lift the top section of dough in both hands and

Arcs

1 Sprinkle work surface with granulated sugar. Roll out the pastry ¼ inch thick into a rectangle.

2 With the length of pastry facing away from you, turn over ½ inch of the pastry edge nearest to you.

3 Holding both hands over the pastry fold, lower them over the fold and roll pastry away from you to form a roll.

Papillons

1 Sprinkle work surface with granulated sugar. Roll out pastry ⅛ inch thick into a rectangle 12 × 8 inches.

2 Cut the pastry into 4 strips, 3 × 8 inches. Brush across the center of 3 strips with lightly beaten egg white.

3 Place 1 dampened pastry strip on top of another dampened strip. Repeat with the third and top with the undampened pastry strip.

carefully fold it towards you, laying it over the two layers. Again, make sure that the edges are aligned and not wavy.

To seal the raw edges, lightly press down with the rolling pin or the side of your little finger approximately three times across the dough. The dough is now ready for a second rolling.

Rolling and refolding. Give the dough a half turn, so that the raw edges are top and bottom. Using the rolling pin, very lightly press the dough down and away from you. Repeat the first rolling process again, until the dough reaches the same dimensions. Fold the pastry rectangle exactly as described before. Finish by sealing the edges with the rolling pin or your finger.

Relaxing the dough. By now, the dough will be in need of a rest, as it has been rolled and folded twice. To relax the dough, place it on a lightly floured plate, cover with plastic wrap, and place in the refrigerator for at least 30 minutes. This resting time allows the fats to become firm; they have become softened during the rolling and folding. It also allows the gluten in the flour time to relax, ready to be rolled and folded again.

4 Using a sharp knife, cut the pastry roll into ¼-inch slices. Rinse a baking sheet with water.

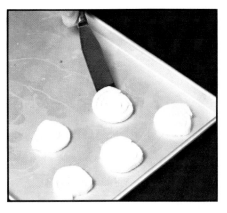

5 Transfer slices to a baking sheet and arrange them 1 inch apart to allow for expansion. Put end slices cut side down.

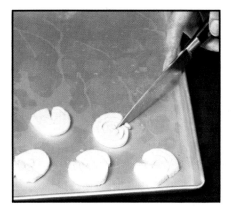

6 Cut each slice from center to outside edge. Separate cut edges slightly, to allow for expansion. Relax for 30 minutes before baking.

4 Turn the pastry; using a sharp knife, cut down through the pastry across the width at ¼-inch intervals.

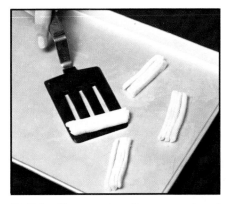

5 Place pastry slices on a rinsed baking sheet, one cut side of the pastry slices facing downwards.

6 Pinch center of each slice to make a butterfly shape. Separate the layers slightly so they will expand. Relax for 30 minutes.

Sacristains and Bow Ties

1 Sprinkle work surface with granulated sugar. Roll out pastry ⅛ inch thick into a rectangle.

2 Brush pastry with lightly beaten egg white to cover the surface. Sprinkle with sliced almonds and granulated sugar.

3 Gently press nuts and sugar into the pastry with the back of a tablespoon. Cut pastry into ¼-inch-wide strips.

Pastry Horns

1 Roll out pastry ⅛ inch thick, into a rectangle approximately 10 × 13 inches. Trim pastry edges straight.

2 Cut pastry into 1-inch-wide strips, each about 12 inches long by the time they are cut.

3 Dampen pastry strips along 1 long side of each strip with water. Take care not to dampen the whole strip.

After this relaxing period, the rolling and folding processes are repeated twice so that the dough is rolled and folded 4 times altogether.

By the end of the fourth rolling and folding, the pastry should be smooth. If for some reason it is still mottled, re-roll once more and relax for a further 30 minutes.

If you are making the pastry in advance, make it up to the final rolling stage and relax in the refrigerator until required. If you do this, however, the longer period in the refrigerator will make it cooler and therefore harder than you require. It will need to stand at room temperature for at least 30 minutes before use.

Making Flaky Pastry

Before you start pastry making, divide the specific quantity of chilled fats called for in your recipe into 4 equal portions. This is necessary because the fats are added to the pastry in 4 stages by 2 different methods. Each method helps to introduce air into the pastry.

Put 3 portions of the butter back into the refrigerator to keep chilled. Sift the flour and salt into a mixing bowl. With a knife, cut the cold fourth portion of fat into small chunks and drop them into the bowl. Use a pastry blender or 2 round-edged knives to cut the fat into

4 To make sacristains hold both ends of each pastry strip and twist in opposite directions, to form corkscrew shapes.

5 To make bow ties hold both ends and give pastry strip a single twist in the center with a corkscrew action.

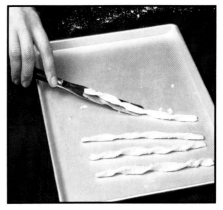

6 Transfer sacristains or bow ties to a rinsed baking sheet, a little apart to allow for expansion. Relax for 30 minutes.

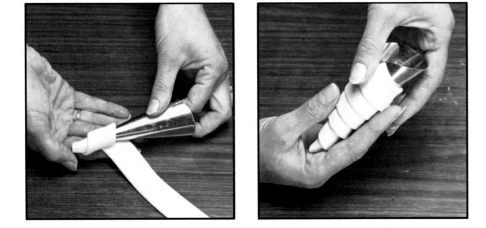

4 Wind pastry strip around an ungreased cornet form, starting at the pointed end. Pastry must overlap the dampened edge.

5 Gently press edges together with fingertips to secure pastry. Place horns on a rinsed baking sheet.

6 Relax pastry horns in the refrigerator for 30 minutes. Brush with required glaze and bake for specified time.

the flour until it is reduced to pea-size particles. With cool fingertips, rub the mixture together until it resembles bread crumbs. Let the crumbs fall back into the bowl. Quickly add the water and optional lemon juice, mixing them so that you get a fairly soft, pliable but not sticky dough. Turn the dough out onto a lightly floured board or work surface and knead it lightly to make a smooth, crack-free dough. Pat the dough into a rectangular shape.

With the dough still on the floured board and using short, even, light strokes, roll the dough to an oblong, three times as long as it is wide, approximately ¼ inch thick. Use a table knife to mark the pastry into 3 equal sections.

Cut the first of the remaining quarters of fat into small pieces. (This will be one quarter of the total amount of butter and one quarter of the total amount of lard used.) Dot the pieces of

fat on the top two thirds of the pastry to within ½ inch of the edge.

Folding and sealing the dough. The dough must now be folded to produce alternate layers of dough and fat. Start by lifting the fatless section of dough carefully with both hands and fold it over the center section of dough. Do not handle the pastry excessively or pull it about clumsily with hot hands as this could make the dough sticky and unmanageable. Just fold it over like the flap of an envelope. The outside edge should be flush with the marked line running through the center of the portion dotted with fat.

Now lift the top section of dough carefully with your hands. Fold it over the top of the other sections, taking care to keep the edges straight. Brush off any excess flour from around the pastry.

The edges of the layers must now be sealed by pressing down lightly with a rolling pin. To do this give the dough a half turn, so that the folds are now at the sides. Lightly seal the 3 raw edges with a rolling pin and press pastry parcel in about 3 places to distribute the air. The pastry may be relaxed briefly in the refrigerator at this point.

Making new layers. Remove the dough and the second quarter of fats from the refrigerator. Repeat the process of dotting on fat, folding and rolling. Be careful not to roll over the edges, as some of the precious air would be lost. If time permits, relax the dough again.

For the final re-rolling, repeat the process with the last of the chilled fats. Fold and roll the dough to seal. Cover the dough loosely with plastic wrap and place in the refrigerator for a minimum of 30 minutes to firm and relax. The resting period makes the pastry easier to handle and also gives a more flaky texture. The more relaxed the pastry, the easier it is to roll, the less the shrinkage during baking, and the more crisp and tender the texture.

After the resting period, roll the pastry into an oblong shape and fold into two. The pastry is now ready to use as required.

Shaping Quick Puff Pastry and Flaky Pastry

Making fancy sweet pastry shapes with quick puff pastry or flaky pastry need not present any problems, even if this is your first attempt. These intricately shaped horns, curls and twists shown can look hard to make if you have never tackled them before or have only

seen them displayed in bakery windows. But the procedures for making them are relatively simple, and the main skills needed are those needed for making the pastry to begin with. Once the pastry has been made and relaxed for 30 minutes, it is ready for rolling and shaping.

Before you place the pastry on the work surface, sprinkle the surface liberally with granulated sugar, which caramelizes during baking. The result is a baked pastry with a rich golden brown color. It also sweetens the pastry and makes it deliciously crisp, even when eaten plain.

A good rule of thumb, when rolling out the pastry, is to sprinkle the rolling surface evenly with about ¼ cup sugar for 1 pound pastry.

Fillings for Dessert Pastries

Classic sweet fillings for *mille-feuilles* and for *tranches* are simple whipped cream, plain or flavored; *crème pâtissière* (pastry cream, see Index for recipe); and buttercream, plain or mousseline (following procedure). Any of these can be combined with fresh fruit. For *mille-feuilles* the fruit should be in thin slices so that it cannot slip from between the layers of pastry. *Tranches* can be filled with fruit alone, arranged decoratively and then coated with a glaze made from warmed and sieved apricot jam or red-currant jelly. However, a *tranche* is often filled first with one of the creams mentioned, with the fruit arranged on top.

One of the most successful fillings is the mousseline buttercream, or *crème au beurre au sucre cuit*, buttercream made with sugar syrup. This is a more involved method of making buttercream, for the egg yolks are almost poached in a hot sugar syrup when the two are beaten together before the butter is added. Because the yolks are cooked rather than raw, the result is a finer cream. It can therefore be made in hot weather without the fear that it will not become firm.

Here is a method for making it: Place 8 ounces unsalted butter in a

makes about 2 cups

8 ounces unsalted butter
1 large egg plus 3 egg yolks, or 5 egg yolks
½ cup granulated sugar
2 tablespoons prepared strong black coffee

 Pour syrup into egg mixture in a steady stream, beating continually by hand or hand-held electric mixer.

warmed mixing bowl. Beat with a wooden spoon or a hand-held electric mixer until the butter is smooth, but not at all melted.

Choose another bowl that will fit over a pan of hot water; or use the top pan of a double boiler. Separate 5 large eggs and drop the eggs into the bowl. If you prefer, you may substitute 1 whole egg for 2 yolks, therefore using 1 whole egg and 3 egg yolks. Do not be tempted to use more than 1 whole egg. Beat

1 Place the butter in a warmed bowl and beat until smooth. Place eggs in another bowl and beat together to blend.

2 Place sugar in a heavy saucepan with 3 tablespoons water and bring to a boil.

3 Boil sugar syrup until the soft-ball stage is reached, 230° to 234°F. Remove pan from heat.

5 Place syrup and egg mixture in top pan of a double boiler. Beat for 4 to 5 minutes, until doubled in volume and foamy.

6 Set top pan of double boiler in a bowl of cold water and beat the mixture until tepid.

7 Beat egg mixture, a spoonful at a time, into creamed butter until it is all incorporated. Finally beat in the coffee.

the yolks, and the whole egg if you are using it.

Place ½ cup sugar in a small heavy saucepan and add 3 tablespoons water. Stir until sugar is dissolved, then bring the syrup to a boil and continue to boil, shaking the saucepan from time to time. The syrup is ready when it reaches the soft-ball stage, 230° to 234°F on a candy thermometer.

When the syrup reaches this stage, pour it onto the yolks in a steady trickle. At the same time beat the egg yolks hard with a whisk or a hand-held electric mixer. When all the syrup has been incorporated in the egg yolks, set the bowl over a pan of hot, but not boiling, water. Continue to beat the syrup and egg yolks for 4 to 5 minutes, until the mixture has doubled in volume and is light and foamy. Make a cold-water bath by filling a large bowl with cold water. Set the bowl contain-

ing the sugar and egg yolks in the cold-water bath, making sure the water is not so high that it spills into the bowl. Continue beating the sugar and egg yolks until the mixture is tepid. (In baking this is called "beating warm and cold.")

Beat the tepid mixture, a spoonful at a time, into the creamed butter, until it has all been incorporated. This mixture should be firm without having to be chilled.

Crème Pâtissière
(Pastry Cream)

makes 2 cups

2	egg yolks
4	tablespoons sugar
1	tablespoon cornstarch
4	teaspoons flour

1¼	cups milk
1	egg white
½	teaspoon vanilla extract

Drop the egg yolks into a mixing bowl and beat lightly with a fork. Add the sugar and beat until the mixture is creamy. Sift in the cornstarch and flour, a little at a time, beating constantly. Gradually mix in 5 tablespoons of the milk. Heat the rest of the milk in a medium-size saucepan over high heat. Remove pan from heat and pour the hot milk into the egg-yolk mixture, beating well with a wire whisk. Return the mixture to the pan and set over moderate heat. Stirring constantly, bring it to a boil. Remove pan from heat and beat until the mixture is smooth. Set it aside and let it become cool.

Beat the egg white in a small bowl until stiff. Transfer about one quarter of the cooled milk mixture to a medium-size bowl. Carefully fold the egg white into the mixture, then fold the egg-white mixture into the rest of the milk mixture in the saucepan. Add the vanilla extract. Return saucepan to very low heat and cook the pastry cream for 2 minutes. Remove pan from heat and cool the pastry cream completely.

Raspberry Palmiers

makes 12

1	pound Puff Pastry (see Index)
	milk or beaten egg
1	cup heavy cream, well chilled

¼	cup granulated sugar
1	teaspoon vanilla extract
2	cups fresh raspberries confectioners' sugar

Use the puff pastry to shape 24 palmiers (see Index). Brush them with milk or beaten egg and bake in a preheated 400°F oven for 10 to 15 minutes, until puffed and golden brown.

Pour the cream into a bowl and add ¼ cup sugar and the vanilla. Whip until the cream just holds its shape. Fill a large piping bag fitted with a star nozzle with the cream and pipe large swirls on one side of 12 cold palmiers. Rinse and hull the raspberries. Arrange the raspberries on top of the cream and top each pastry with another palmier, pressing it down lightly. Sift a little confectioners' sugar over the top of each pastry.

Variations: Use strawberries instead of raspberries. Omit sugar and vanilla from the whipped cream and substitute 2 tablespoons Cointreau liqueur. When cream is whipped, fold in ¼ cup drained chopped mandarin orange segments or the chopped pulp of 1 large orange. Roll the pastry in brown sugar instead of granulated and sprinkle the palmiers with chopped mixed nuts. Serve them singly, without a filling.

Gâteau Pithiviers

6 to 8 portions

1	pound Puff Pastry (see Index)
3	ounces blanched almonds
½	cup superfine sugar

2	tablespoons unsalted butter
2	large egg yolks
2	tablespoons dark rum
1	egg, beaten

Preheat oven to 400°F. Dampen a baking sheet. Divide the pastry into 2 slightly unequal pieces. Roll each piece to a circle about 9 inches in diameter. Make one circle slightly thinner than the other.

Put the almonds in a mortar and pound to a paste with a pestle; or pulverize in a food processor. Gradually cream 6 tablespoons of the sugar and the butter into the almond paste. Gradually work in the egg yolks and rum. Beat the paste until it is white and fluffy.

Place the thinner circle of pastry on the baking sheet. Spread the almond cream over it, leaving about ½ inch of clear pastry at the edge all around. Place the other circle of pastry on top. Using a sharp knife, mark a cartwheel pattern on top. Brush the top with beaten egg and sprinkle with remaining superfine sugar. Bake in the center of the oven for 25 to 30 minutes, until golden brown.

Chantilly Fruit Tartlets

makes 12

½ pound Flaky Pastry (see Index)
3 tablespoons red-currant jelly

8 ounces soft fruit: strawberries, raspberries, blueberries
½ cup heavy cream
few drops of vanilla extract

Preheat oven to 425°F. Move the shelf to the top third of the oven.

Roll out the pastry ¼ inch thick and cut into 12 circles slightly larger than the tartlet pans you plan to use. Carefully line the tartlet pans with the pastry circles, pressing them in and making the edges even. Cut circles of baking parchment or foil slightly larger than the tartlet pans. Place the linings on the pastry and fill with dried beans or ceramic pellets. Bake blind for 10 minutes. Remove linings and beans and return tartlet pans to the oven for 10 minutes longer. Remove from oven and leave in the pans to cool for 3 minutes.

Carefully remove pastry cases from the pans, place on a wire rack, and leave to cool completely. Place the red-currant jelly in a small saucepan and beat with a wooden spoon. Heat it gently until jelly melts. Remove from heat and sieve the jelly. Prepare the chosen fruit.

Put the cream and vanilla extract in a bowl and whip until the cream holds its shape. Pipe or spoon the cream into the tartlet cases. Arrange the fruit on top of the cream. Brush the melted jelly over the fruit and serve immediately.

Tranche aux Fruits

(Fruit Tart Strip)

8 to 10 portions

1 pound Puff Pastry (see Index)	1 cup green grapes
1 egg, beaten	1 cup strawberries
1 cup heavy cream	1 large ripe peach
1 banana	3 tablespoons apricot jam

Preheat oven to 400°F. Dampen a baking sheet. Roll out the pastry to a rectangle 7 × 12 inches. With a sharp knife cut away a border of pastry 1½ inches wide all around the rectangle. Lift it off. Roll out the solid rectangle to its original size, before the border was cut. Brush the edges of the rectangle with beaten egg. Lift the base onto the dampened baking sheet and place the cutout border on top. Press the edges lightly to seal. Brush the top of the border piece with beaten egg. Bake for 30 minutes, until pastry is golden and puffed up. Cool on a wire rack.

Whip the cream until it holds its shape. Fill the *tranche* with the cream, smoothing it to make an even layer. Peel and slice the banana. Peel and seed the grapes. Wash, hull, and halve the strawberries. Peel, pit, and slice the peach. Arrange the fruits decoratively over the cream to cover it completely.

Heat the apricot jam over low heat until liquid, then put through a sieve. Spoon the sieved jam over the fruit. Allow the glaze to set before serving the fruit strip.

Cinnamon Chocolate Tart

6 portions

½ pound Flaky Pastry (see Index)
2 ounces (2 squares) semisweet chocolate
4 tablespoons unsalted butter
¼ cup sugar

2 eggs, separated
½ teaspoon ground cinnamon
⅓ cup ground blanched almonds
¾ cup plain cake crumbs
pinch of salt

Preheat oven to 400°F. Roll out the pastry to fit an 8-inch flan ring placed on a baking sheet. Line the ring with the pastry and chill for 15 minutes.

Line the pastry with parchment paper or foil and fill with dried beans or ceramic pellets. Bake for 10 minutes. Remove dried beans and lining; bake for 3 to 5 minutes longer, until pastry is just set. Remove baking sheet and flan ring from the oven. Reduce oven temperature to 350°F.

Melt the chocolate in the top pan of a double boiler over hot, not boiling, water. Cream the butter and sugar together in a large bowl until light and fluffy. Beat egg yolks together; add to the creamed mixture, a little at a time, beating well after each addition. Beat the melted chocolate into the creamed mixture. Stir in cinnamon, almonds and cake crumbs; mix well.

Add a pinch of salt to the egg whites; beat until stiff but not dry. Carefully fold the egg whites into the chocolate filling. Turn the filling into the pastry shell. Bake for 20 minutes.

Serve the tart hot with custard sauce, or cold with light cream.

Apricot and Almond Buttercream Horns

makes 8 to 10

1 pound Puff Pastry (see Index)
milk
½ cup granulated sugar
6 ounces unsalted butter, softened
¾ cup confectioners' sugar
2 large egg yolks

2 tablespoons apricot brandy, or 1 teaspoon vanilla extract
3 tablespoons apricot preserves or jam
2 tablespoons chopped blanched almonds

Roll out the pastry, cut into strips, and wind them around *cornet* (horn) forms as described under Pastry Horns (see Index). Brush the pastry with milk and sprinkle each one lightly with granulated sugar. Bake for 15 to 20 minutes, until pastry is puffed and golden brown. Allow pastries to cool for 5 minutes before carefully removing the forms. Transfer horns to a cooling rack and leave until completely cold.

Make the buttercream filling: Place the softened butter in a warmed mixing bowl and beat it until smooth. Sift ½ cup confectioners' sugar into the butter, then add the egg yolks and brandy or vanilla. Beat with an electric mixer at moderate speed for 2 minutes. Or beat the ingredients with a wooden spoon for 5 minutes, until the mixture is smooth and creamy. If the filling has become too soft during beating, chill it.

Drop a small spoonful of apricot preserves into the bottom of each pastry horn and sprinkle a few chopped almonds on the preserves. Fill the horns to the top with the buttercream filling and place pastries on a wire rack. Sift a little confectioners' sugar over the pastries and transfer them to a serving plate.

Variations: Omit apricot preserves, nuts and liqueur and fold up to 1 cup hulled and quartered strawberries into the buttercream. Fill the horns with the fruit and buttercream mixture, then top each horn with a whole fresh strawberry.

Omit brandy or vanilla from the buttercream and use instead 2 ounces melted chocolate, rum to taste and ¼ cup seedless raisins.

Peach and Banana Puffs

makes 8

4 small fresh peaches, or 8 canned peach halves, drained
1 cup dry white wine, or syrup from canned peaches (both optional)
3 tablespoons lemon juice
1 teaspoon ground allspice

scant ¼ cup soft brown sugar
1 pound Quick Puff Pastry (see Index)
1 large banana
1 egg white, beaten
superfine sugar

If using fresh fruit, peel, pit and halve the peaches. Pour the wine or the same quantity of water into a skillet or large saucepan. Add 2 tablespoons lemon juice, the ground allspice and brown sugar. Stir once, then bring to a boil. Simmer for about 2 minutes, until sugar has dissolved completely. Remove pan from heat and add the fresh peach halves. Reduce heat, cover the skillet, and simmer for 10 to 15 minutes, until peaches are just tender. Uncover the pan and set aside until fruit is completely cold.

Carefully lift out the peaches with a slotted spoon and pat them dry on paper towels. Reserve the poaching liquid. If using canned peaches, drain them, reserving the syrup.

Preheat oven to 400°F. Place the rack in the top third of the oven.

Cut the pastry into 2 equal pieces with a sharp knife. Roll out each piece of pastry to ⅛-inch thickness. Cut out 8 fluted 3-inch circles from 1 piece of the pastry. Cut out 8 fluted 4-inch circles from the second piece of pastry. Layer the trimmings on top of one another and roll out to ⅛-inch thickness. Use a very small fancy cutter to cut out 24 fancy shapes from the trimmings, and reserve them.

Peel the banana and cut into 24 thin slices. Place the slices in a bowl and sprinkle with remaining lemon juice. Toss banana slices to coat with lemon juice.

Place the 8 smaller pastry circles on a baking sheet and brush the edges with a little beaten egg white. Place 3 slices of banana, overlapping, in the center of each pastry circle. Place a peach half, cavity side down, on top of the banana. Cover each peach with a large circle of pastry. Press the edges together to seal. Brush the top surface of each pie with a little beaten egg white. Arrange 3 fancy pastry shapes on top of each one. Brush the decorations with egg white and sprinkle with a little superfine sugar. Bake for 20 to 25 minutes, until pastry is puffed and golden brown.

Transfer puffs to a wire cake rack. Serve hot with the poaching liquid thickened with arrowroot, or cold with cream.

Variations: Use apricots instead of peaches and add a little Amaretto (almond liqueur) to the poaching liquid or syrup. Place a small ball of marzipan in each peach cavity before baking.

Eccles Cakes

makes 16

1 pound Puff Pastry (see Index)
2 tablespoons butter or margarine
1 tablespoon soft brown sugar

4 ounces dried currants
2 ounces candied fruit peel
½ teaspoon allspice
milk
superfine sugar

Roll out the pastry to ⅛-inch thickness and cut into sixteen 3½-inch circles. Roll the pastry circles lightly with a rolling pin to make them slightly larger. Place butter or margarine in a small saucepan and add brown sugar, currants, candied peel and spice. Heat over low heat until butter has melted, then stir to mix together.

Dampen the edges of the pastry circles with a little milk and place a heaping teaspoon of the filling in the center of each circle. Using your fingertips, gather up the pastry edges over the filling and pinch together to seal. Turn the cakes over so that the sealed part is underneath. Gently flatten each cake with the palm of your hand. Place cakes on a rinsed baking sheet and place in the refrigerator for 20 minutes to relax the pastry.

Preheat oven to 425°F. Place the rack in the top third of the oven.

Use a sharp knife to make 3 parallel slits across the top of each cake. Brush with milk and sprinkle with a little super-fine sugar. Bake the cakes for 20 to 25 minutes, until cakes are puffed and golden.

Part Five

CELEBRATION LUNCHEON

For people who love to cook and eat, almost anything is cause for culinary celebration: a birthday, Valentine's day, a job promotion, the anniversary of something special in your life (a marriage? your dog's birthday?), visits from faraway friends. The following menu not only says "you're special" because extra time and work are involved, but it is also a perfect meal for the servantless household, because so much can be prepared ahead and assembled at the last minute.

The cherry tomatoes can be scooped out a day ahead and refrigerated, along with the *pesto.* The filling can be assembled and the tomatoes filled an hour or two before the celebration. The vegetable terrine can be made as much as a week ahead and kept tightly covered in the refrigerator; indeed, the flavors tend to intensify upon keeping. The racks of lamb can be boned (by you or the butcher) 2 or 3 days ahead. The bones are then used to make the bordelaise sauce, which actually gets better a few days after it is made. The buttery orzo pasta (or rice, if the rice-shaped pasta is difficult to find) should be made just before serving and so should the spinach, which is tossed in a hot pan with the oil and butter exactly as you would toss a salad. The pastry horns, which any Anglophile will recognize as part and parcel of a hearty English country tea, are filled with *our* version of Devonshire cream—whipped sweet cream mixed with a dab of sour cream and enriched with a dash of brandy—and some sliced strawberries and blueberries. The horns can be made ahead and filled just before the guests sit down to lunch, or, if you enjoy preparing foods in front of guests, they can be filled with a flourish at table. If the strawberry season is upon us you may choose to gild the lily with strawberries dipped into chocolate, an easy but impressive sight: Simply melt some good semisweet chocolate in the top pan of a double boiler over hot water, and pour it into a warm bowl. Bring the bowl and the strawberries to the table and let each guest dip his own. A thimble of iced brandy or Kirsch is another lily-gilder. Keep the liqueur in the freezer and it will be almost syrupy and very easy on the palate.

Dressing your table, like dressing yourself and your house, is an art. Will you opt for a strictly formal look with white damask and napkins, fine china, a formal flower arrangement? Or would you prefer to create a mood with informal accessories? Use red bandanna "placemats" and napkins,

mounds of vegetables in straw, colorful china for a farmhouse look. Your centerpiece may be a profusion of exotic orchids, masses of colorful field flowers, or interestingly arranged seaweeds. Whatever the look you decide on, carry the theme through with every aspect of your table decorations. Heavy, old silver flatware transcends all, but it might look awkward to have inexpensive plastic-handled cutlery while using Limoges china and Baccarat crystal. So be consistent, knowing that this meal contains foods that do well in both a formal and an informal setting.

Champagne

Champagne says celebration to everyone, and this is one beverage that is acceptable from appetizer to dessert. Champagnes and sparkling wines come in all price ranges. True French Champagne is produced only in the Champagne region; other sparkling wines are called *mousseux* or sparkling wine. Champagne comes in varying sweetnesses: *brut* or *nature* is very, very dry; *extra-sec* is fairly dry; *sec* is medium-sweet; *demi-sec* is quite sweet; *doux* is sweet. The

best Champagnes, also the most expensive, carry a vintage date and are usually dry. Nonvintage wines, which are made from grapes of several years, are less costly, but may be pleasant wines nonetheless. If you are celebrating a birthday or anniversary, it is fun to serve a Champagne from that year, though a magnum of Bollinger 1947 might set you back a few pennies. But any effervescent sparkling wine, white, red or rosé, is perceived by most people as a "celebration" drink.

CELEBRATION LUNCHEON FOR SIX

Cherry Tomatoes Filled with Pesto
Creamy Vegetable Terrine
Lamb Noisettes with Bordelaise Sauce
Orzo with Parsley
Stir-Fried Spinach
Cream Horns

Wine Suggestion: Champagne

MARKET LIST

Meat and Fish

2 large racks of lamb
1 beef marrowbone

Fruit and Vegetables

24 cherry tomatoes, about 2 pints
8 ounces green snap beans
3 carrots
4 fresh artichokes, or 1 can artichoke bottoms
10 ounces frozen peas
2 pounds fresh spinach

2 leeks
1 onion
1 large bunch of fresh basil
2 bunches of parsley
1 bunch of green onions (scallions)
1 bunch of fresh dill
1 bunch of fresh mint

2 navel oranges
1 lemon
½ pint blueberries
1 pint strawberries
2 ounces pine nuts or shelled walnuts
1 pound orzo (rice-shaped pasta)

Staples

cream cheese
Brie cheese
Parmesan cheese
butter
heavy cream
sour cream
eggs

olive oil
peanut oil
chicken stock
beef stock
white wine
red wine
brandy

unflavored gelatin (6 envelopes)
garlic
tomato juice
granulated sugar
flour
Dijon-style mustard

Tabasco
salt
black, white and cayenne pepper
bay leaf
dried thyme

Cherry Tomatoes Filled with Pesto

6 portions

24 firm cherry tomatoes

3 ounces cream cheese

Pesto

2 cups fresh basil leaves, without stems

½ cup parsley leaves, without stems

2 garlic cloves

¼ cup pine nuts or shelled walnuts

¼ cup grated Parmesan cheese

⅓ cup olive oil
salt and pepper

Prepare tomatoes: With a small sharp knife cut off the tops of the tomatoes and reserve tops for another use. Carefully loosen the insides of the tomatoes and scoop out with a small spoon or the small end of a melon baller. (The insides of the tomatoes and the tops can be blended for great-tasting tomato juice.) Turn tomatoes upside down to drain on a paper towel. If prepared in advance, refrigerate them in this manner.

Place cream cheese in a bowl and let it soften to room temperature. Mash it with a fork. Make the *pesto:* Combine basil and parsley in the container of a food processor or blender. Peel garlic cloves, chop, and add to the herbs along with pine nuts, Parmesan cheese and olive oil. Blend or process until almost smooth; the mixture should remain a little chunky. Taste and season. Combine *pesto* and cream cheese, mixing well with a fork. Use about 1 teaspoon of this mixture to stuff each tomato. Refrigerate tomatoes for several hours, then let them stand at room temperature for about 30 minutes before serving.

Creamy Vegetable Terrine

6 to 8 portions

Vegetable Layer

8 ounces green snap beans

3 carrots

4 cooked artichoke bottoms

10 ounces frozen peas
dash of Tabasco
salt and white pepper

5 envelopes (¼ ounce each) unflavored gelatin

1¼ cups dry white wine

3½ cups defatted rich chicken stock

Creamy Layer

1	envelope (¼ ounce) unflavored gelatin
¼	cup cold water
1	garlic clove
6	ounces Brie cheese, with rind on
2	tablespoons white wine
1	cup dairy sour cream

2	tablespoons Dijon-style mustard
2	tablespoons minced green onions (scallions)
1	tablespoon snipped fresh dill
	pinch of cayenne pepper

Wash and trim green beans and cut into ½-inch diagonal slices. Scrape carrots and cut into thin rounds. Steam all the vegetables until just tender; drain and toss with Tabasco and a pinch each of salt and white pepper. Chill a bread pan or meat-loaf pan, 9 × 5 × 3 inches, in the refrigerator. Soften the gelatin in the wine; set over low heat until gelatin is melted and the mixture is clear. Add cold stock, mix, and pour half of the mixture into the chilled mold. Chill until gelatin is set.

Arrange part of the vegetables in an attractive pattern over the set gelatin. Carefully pour a ½-inch layer of gelatin over the vegetables and refrigerate until set.

Assemble the ingredients for the creamy layer. Soften the gelatin in the water in a small pan, then place over low heat until gelatin is dissolved. Peel garlic and put through a press. Put all the ingredients, including the dissolved gelatin, in a blender or food processor and process until smooth. When the vegetable layer is set, pour in part of the creamy mixture and let it set. Continue alternating vegetables, liquid gelatin and creamy mixture until all ingredients are used and the mold is filled. After pouring in each layer, refrigerate until that layer is set. Refrigerate the finished mold overnight.

To unmold, run a knife around the edge of the pan. Place an oval platter on top and invert platter and pan together. Place a towel wrung out in very hot water on the bottom of the pan for a few seconds and the jellied mold should slip out. Cut into slices to serve.

Lamb Noisettes with Bordelaise Sauce

6 portions

2	large racks of lamb, about 3 pounds each
2	slices of prosciutto
2	leeks
2	tablespoons oil
2	tablespoons butter
¼	cup dry red wine

	salt and pepper
1½	cups Bordelaise Sauce (recipe follows)
1	bunch of fresh mint
2	navel oranges, peeled and sliced

Have the racks of lamb boned. Be sure butcher gives you the bones as they will be needed for the sauce. Dice the prosciutto. Wash leeks carefully, splitting them to the root end if necessary to remove all sand. Chop the white part only into small pieces. Heat oil and butter in a large saucepan. Brown the pieces of lamb in the pan, turning them to brown all sides. Add diced prosciutto and chopped leeks and brown them also. Pour in the wine, cover the pan, and simmer for 12 minutes, until lamb is done to your taste; it should still be slightly pink in the center. The meat of the rack is thin and tender, so do not overcook it. Season meat lightly with salt and pepper. Remove lamb to a cutting board and cut into slices or chunks, making 6 to 8 pieces from each rack. Heat the mixture remaining in the saucepan with the bordelaise sauce, and serve the sauce with the lamb. Garnish with orange slices and mint.

Bordelaise Sauce

about 2 cups

1	beef marrowbone
1	medium-size onion
2	tablespoons butter
2	tablespoons flour
3	cups beef stock

	lamb bones from boned racks
1	bay leaf
	small pinch of dried thyme
1	cup dry red wine
¼	cup tomato juice

Have the marrowbone sawed into sections. Peel and mince the onion. Melt the butter in a large saucepan and sauté the onion until tender and translucent. Stir in the flour and mix well. Add beef stock, lamb bones, marrowbone pieces, herbs and liquids. Bring to a boil, lower heat, cover, and simmer for 1 hour.

Strain the sauce into a clean saucepan and reduce it over moderate heat to 2 cups. Remove marrow from the sections of bone and cut into small dice; add to the sauce. Any sauce not used for this dinner may be frozen.

Orzo with Parsley

6 portions

2 cups orzo	¾ cup chopped fresh parsley, without stems
2 teaspoons salt	1 garlic clove
6 tablespoons butter	

Bring a large pot of water to a boil and drop in the orzo and the salt. Cook for about 10 minutes, until done to your taste. Drain and return to the warm pot. Stir in the butter and parsley. Peel garlic and put through a press into the pasta. Toss to combine well and keep warm until serving time.

Stir-Fried Spinach

6 portions

2 pounds fresh spinach	2 tablespoons peanut oil
2 garlic cloves	juice of 1 lemon
3 tablespoons butter	

Wash spinach carefully and pull off stems; drain well. Peel and chop garlic. In a wok or large skillet melt the butter with the oil. Toss the drained spinach in the hot butter and oil until just beginning to wilt. Mix in garlic and lemon juice, toss, and serve immediately.

Cream Horns

8 pastries

8 ounces prepared Puff Pastry (see Volume 4 Index)	3 cups heavy cream
	½ cup dairy sour cream
2 egg whites	¼ cup brandy
2 teaspoons water	1 cup blueberries
½ cup granulated sugar	1 cup sliced strawberries

Roll out puff pastry ⅛ inch thick. Cut the pastry into 6-inch strips. Have ready 8 metal horn molds or cornucopias made from heavy foil. Wind the pastry strips around the horn molds. Make sure the edges of the strips overlap and seal them well. Stop the dough ½ inch from the top of the molds to facilitate removal of the tubes. Chill for 1 hour.

Preheat oven to 350°F. Beat the egg whites with the water and brush the mixture over the pastry. Roll the pastry in granulated sugar. Place the horns on ungreased baking sheets and bake for 45 minutes, until pastry is golden. Remove molds immediately by gently twisting them free.

Make the cream filling: Whip the cream and stir in the sugar remaining from rolling the pastry horns. Add sour cream and brandy. Just before serving, stir in the blueberries and strawberries, and fill the mixture into the pastry horns.

INDEX